Everything is Figureoutable

'Millions of young women look to Marie as their inspiration for empowerment and achievement . . . She's the thought leader for the next generation'

Oprah Winfrey

'*Everything is Figureoutable* is a whirlwind of power, humour, pragmatism and grace. Marie Forleo writes exactly the way she lives – with full-on enthusiasm, no-bullshit directness and a ferocious commitment to self-accountability. This woman is the real deal, people. This book will change lives'

Liz Gilbert, author of *Eat, Pray, Love* and *Big Magic*

'*Everything is Figureoutable* will revolutionize your life. Whatever you're working on, dreaming of, or even avoiding, the solution is spelled out here. And if you're thinking "but I can't", you *especially* need to stop reading this blurb and just buy the book already, because as Marie will show you through the inspiring stories and practical tools in these power-packed pages, you CAN!'

Sarah Jones, Tony® and Obie Award-winning performer and writer

'What does it take to make a reader feel loved, inspired and called out on their BS all at the same time? I don't know, but Marie Forleo has figured it out! Smart, funny and as brilliant as it is straightforward. LOVED it!'

Brené Brown, PhD, author of *Dare to Lead* and *Daring Greatly*

'Here's the divine Marie Forleo with a book that is both a comfort and provocation. No matter what . . . you can do this!! The wisdom in this book will make you see yourself and your potential through a thrilling new lens'

Dani Shapiro, number one *New York Times* bestselling author of *Inheritance*

'The best books fit our persistent locks like a perfectly made key. Marie is honest, generous and caring, and she's sharing her wisdom here. If you're looking for the next step on your journey to make a difference for others, here it is'

Seth Godin, author of *This is Marketing*

'*Everything is Figureoutable* is a must-read for anyone who wants to face their fears, fulfil their dreams and find a better way forward. With humour and insight, Marie Forleo offers practical advice about how to get it done. This book delivers a knock-out punch to whatever is holding you back'

Cheryl Strayed, author of *Wild*

'Marie Forleo – always the first to jump in and champion other women – is an inspiration to me. With *Everything is Figureoutable* she gives us the best of a leadership book and the best of self-help. It's hilarious, relatable and actionable. I finished the last page on fire to implement Marie's tools into my personal and work life'

Abby Wambach, number one *New York Times* bestselling
author of *Wolfpack*, Olympian, activist

'Most of us think of Marie Forleo as a performer, mentor, role model for a generation of young women and men, and hostess of *MarieTV*. *Everything is Figureoutable* will change that. The lady can write. *Everything is Figureoutable* is a dazzling manifesto on self-belief and self-empowerment. Perhaps her greatest contribution yet'

Steven Pressfield, bestselling author of
The War of Art and *The Artist's Journey*

'Thanks to Marie Forleo, "Everything is figureoutable" has been one of my mantras – and her book delivers on its promise. Marie's guidance is brilliant and illuminating, and she delivers it in the most heartfelt, down-to-earth way. *Everything is Figureoutable* will energize you, move you and inspire you to take fearless action!'

Gabrielle Bernstein, number one *New York Times*
bestselling author of *The Universe Has Your Back*

'Marie Forleo is a force of nature, out there helping others find their own confidence to grow themselves and their businesses. In *Everything is Figureoutable*, Marie shares some of the most powerful lessons she has learned'

Simon Sinek, optimist and *New York Times* bestselling
author of *Start with Why* and *Leaders Eat Last*

'I'm a long-time fan of *MarieTV*, and this book represents everything I adore about Marie – as a teacher, a woman and an overall badass! From her personal story and mantra to the tales of lives she's inspired and changed for the better, Marie offers up her real-talk insights with candour, generosity and immense wisdom, all with her inimitable style of Forleo fun!'

Bryce Dallas Howard, actor and director

'The *Everything is Figureoutable* belief system is a life-saver, life-changer, a belief system for the ages. Every parent should start with this on how to raise their kids to be happy and self-sufficient. *Everything is Figureoutable* will shatter your limitations, open your heart and help you reach your most long-buried dreams'

David Bach, nine-times *New York Times* bestselling author of
The Latte Factor and *Smart Women Finish Rich*

'This is a fantastic book. It's a delight to read plus it's overflowing with powerful ideas and tools. Marie is so warm and wonderful. It's like talking with your best friend who also happens to be incredibly wise, helpful – and funny!'

Rick Hanson, PhD, author of *Resilient: How to Grow an Unshakable Core of Calm, Strength and Happiness*

'*Everything is Figureoutable* is an unapologetic guide to solving your biggest problems and accomplishing your wildest dreams'

Sophia Amoruso, co-founder and CEO, Girlboss

'I have often marvelled at the creativity, intensity and integrity with which Marie builds her career. I've wondered: how does she do so much so well? In *Everything is Figureoutable*, Marie reveals to her readers every secret and strategy she's used to build her fascinating life and her world-changing platform. This book is exactly like Marie: fast-paced, generous, wise, raw, funny, practical and helpful'

Glennon Doyle, number-one *New York Times* bestselling author of *Love, Warrior*, founder of Together Rising

'This book will change your life in all the best ways possible. Marie, in her straight-up hilarious manner, makes you understand the power that you truly have when you get out of your own damn way, put insight into action and do the work. Her advice has helped me figure out how to live the life of my dreams. *Everything is Figureoutable* will do the same for you'

Becky Lynch, WWE RAW and Inaugural SmackDown Women's Champion

'For centuries, we curious, hungry, joy-seeking humans have been on a quest to un-lock our greatest potential. Well, what if it's easier than we think, and it all starts with one powerful belief? You hold in your hand the key to creating the magical, meaningful life you desire. *Everything is Figureoutable* is a provocative, profound, laugh-your-ass-off game-changer. Devour this book and get busy living! Thank you, Marie Forleo – you are a gift!'

Kris Carr, *New York Times* bestselling author

'Debt, stress, depression, addiction, boring job. It's easy to be paralysed by the enor-mity of life's problems. Despair no more, Marie Forleo's *Everything is Figureoutable* is here. Marie channels her mother's can-do-it mentality into a book that will change your mindset. There is no challenge too small or too great to overcome. You can fix your washing machine and you can launch your dream company. I am often in awe of Marie and everything she has accomplished. And now we have the ACTION-ABLE roadmap on how she does it. Lucky us!'

Jeff Krasno, CEO, Commune

'If you're stuck or frustrated with any aspect of your life, take heart. With her trade-mark mix of warmth, intelligence and insightful advice, Marie Forleo shows us how, as the title says, everything is figureoutable'

Arianna Huffington, Founder and CEO, Thrive Global

'In my world, there are two types of people: those I can trust to figure out a problem and those I can't. Guess which ones I want to work with? *Everything is Figureoutable* gives you the courage to stand strong and find a way forward, no matter what. A must-read!'

Daymond John, co-star of four-time Emmy Award-winning *Shark Tan*

Everything

is

Figureoutable

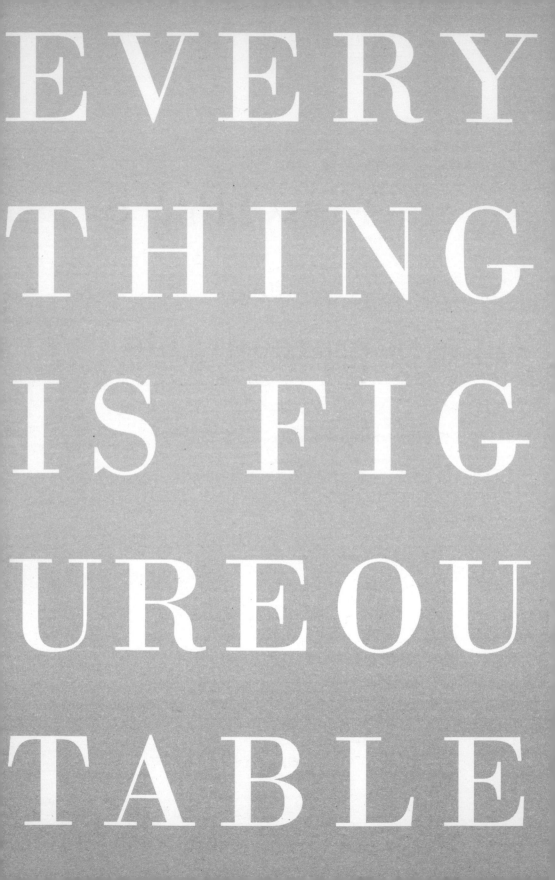

EVERY
THING
IS FIG
UREOU
TABLE

Everything

is

Figureoutable

MARIE FORLEO

BUSINESS

PENGUIN BUSINESS

UK | USA | Canada | Ireland | Australia
India | New Zealand | South Africa

Penguin Business is part of the Penguin Random House group of companies
whose addresses can be found at global.penguinrandomhouse.com.

First published in the United States of America by Portfolio Penguin 2019
First published in Great Britain by Penguin Business 2019
001

Printed and bound in Great Britain by Clays Ltd, Elcograf S.p.A.

A CIP catalogue record for this book is available from the British Library

ISBN: 978–0–241–34103–2

Follow us on LinkedIn: linkedin.com/company/penguinbusiness

www.greenpenguin.co.uk

Penguin Random House is committed to a
sustainable future for our business, our readers
and our planet. This book is made from Forest
Stewardship Council® certified paper.

For my parents.

Thank you for raising me to be

playful, fiercely independent,

and to honor the value

of hard-ass work.

The power isn't out there,

it's in you.

CONTENTS

1

The Tropicana Orange

The obvious is that which is never seen until someone expresses it simply.

Kahlil Gibran

My mother has the tenacity of a bulldog, looks like June Cleaver, and curses like a truck driver. She grew up the daughter of two alcoholic parents in the projects of Newark, New Jersey. She learned, by necessity, how to stretch a dollar bill around the block and is one of the most resourceful and industrious people you could ever meet. She once told me she rarely felt valued, loved, or beautiful, but she held tight to the promise she made to herself that, once she was old enough, she'd find a way to a better life.

As a kid, I remember going through the Sunday paper together and cutting coupons. She taught me all the different ways to save money. She also taught me to pay close attention to the free stuff that brands would send you—like recipe books or cooking utensils—if you saved up and mailed in a "proof of purchase." One of my mom's most prized possessions was a little transistor radio she got from Tropicana orange juice, for free. The radio was the size, color, and shape of an orange, with a red-and-white-striped antenna sticking out the side like a straw. She loved that little radio.

My mom is one of those people who is constantly busy. As a little girl, I knew I could find her somewhere around the house or yard by listening for the tinny sound coming out of that Tropicana orange. One day I was walking home from school and heard the radio playing off in the distance. As I got closer, I realized the music was coming from above. I looked up and saw my mom perched on the roof of our two-story house. "Moooom! Is everything okay? What are you doing all the way up there?!"

She yelled down, "I'm fine, Ree. The roof had a leak. When I called the roofer, he said it would be at least five hundred bucks, probably more. That's friggin' nuts! I remembered seeing some extra asphalt in the garage and figured it would just take a few minutes to fix it up."

Another time, I came home from school and heard the radio buzzing from the back of the house. Mom was in the bathroom, surrounded by tools and exposed pipes. Dust particles filled the air. *"Mom, what's going on?!"*

"Oh, I'm just retiling the bathroom," she said. "I saw a few cracks and didn't want it all to get moldy."

You've got to understand, my mom is high school educated and this was the 1980s. It was a pre-internet, pre-YouTube, pre-Google world. I never knew where I'd find her or what she'd be doing, but all I had to do was follow the crackle of that radio.

One fall day, I came home late from school and something was different. Everything was dark. There was an unusual silence. Something was wrong. I quietly walked through the house afraid of what I might find. Where was the sound of the Tropicana orange? Where was my mom? Then I heard clicks and clacks. I followed that sound and saw my mom huddled over the kitchen table. It looked like an operating room. I saw electrical tape and screwdrivers, and spread out in front of her were countless tiny pieces of a dismantled Tropicana orange radio. "Mom, are you okay? What happened to your radio? Is it broken?"

"It's fine, Ree. No big deal. The antenna got busted and the tuner dial was a little off, so I'm fixing it."

I stood there for a second, watching her work her magic. Finally, I asked, "Hey, Mom, how do you know how to do so many different things that you've never done before, without anyone showing you how to do it?"

She put down her screwdriver, turned to me, and said, "Don't be silly, Ree. Nothing in life is that complicated. You can do whatever you set your mind to if you just roll up your sleeves, get in there, and do it. Everything is figureoutable."

I was transfixed, reveling in and repeating those words in my head: *Everything is figureoutable. Everything is figureoutable. Holy shit, yes . . .*

Everything Is Figureoutable!

This phrase and philosophy took root in my soul. Since then, it's become the most powerful driving force in my life.

It helped me end a physically abusive relationship. In college, it helped me win highly competitive and rare work-study positions to pay for room and board and get into the exact classes I wanted—despite prerequisite policies and wait lists. Even as a kid, it's why I kept trying out for sports and cheer teams, even after getting rejected year after year.

It's helped me land every job I've ever had, from bartending at the most coveted restaurants in Manhattan to lucrative oddball gigs— selling glow sticks at megaclubs—to trading on the floor of the New

York Stock Exchange, publishing at Condé Nast, teaching hip-hop, starring in workout videos, producing and choreographing on MTV, and becoming one of the world's first Nike Elite Dance athletes—despite no formal dance training. It's helped me climb out of debilitating debt, extricate myself from dead-end relationships, and save my most precious ones, often in record time.

It's what gave me the audacity to start a business at twenty-three and build it into a multimillion-dollar, socially conscious education and media company from the ground up—with no clue, experience, investors, graduate degree, or connections. It's what fueled me to start filming videos using my first-generation webcam, which would later evolve into an award-winning online show seen by tens of millions of fans in 195 countries. I don't say this to brag. I say this because deep in my bones I am *that* certain everything really is figureoutable.

Yes, even if you're starting from scratch. Even if you've already tried and failed. Even if you don't have a clue what the hell you're doing or why things keep going wrong. Even if the world has told you time and time again that you can't. Even if you've been born into extraordinary challenges or find yourself with the deck stacked against you.

Maybe you're wondering whether this idea can help you confront a harrowing reality. Like when you're in the midst of despair or a sense of endless futility. Experiences like:

- A frightening and life-altering diagnosis
- The tragic loss of a child or loved one
- Mental illness and recovery after abuse

Yes. *Everything is figureoutable* helps us face hard truths consciously. Throughout this book, you'll hear triumphant tales of everyday people confronting loss, illness, and heart-wrenching pain. These "Figure-outable Field Notes" illustrate how this one simple idea helps us find resilience, resourcefulness, and hope—especially when we need it most.

No matter what you're facing, you have what it takes to figure anything out and become the person you're meant to be.

Despite what society, your family, or your mind may have led you to believe, you are *not* broken. Nothing is intrinsically wrong with you. You're not a mistake, or a fraud, or a fake. You're not weak or incapable.

Quite simply, none of us were given an owner's manual at birth. Our educational system doesn't train us to harness the power of our thoughts, beliefs, emotions, and the wisdom of our bodies. It doesn't teach us how to develop winning mindsets, perspectives, and practical habits not only to meet and overcome life's challenges but also to experience real joy and fulfillment. It fails to show us how much intrinsic power we all have. Sadly, we get very little (if any) practical training on how to use our gifts to make a difference.

It's up to us to fix that, here and now. As the great Maya Angelou said, "Do the best you can until you know better. Then when you know better, do better." Which is why I'm thrilled you're here. Because this book will help you do both.

WHY IT'S IMPORTANT YOU'RE READING THIS NOW

Everything is figureoutable will change your life. You can use it to solve mundane problems like a busted washing machine or a flat tire. You can use it to build a company, reshape your health, or create financial freedom. You can use it to save (or end) a relationship or create the most magnificent, passionate love story of your dreams. You can use it to find your way out of chronic stress, grief, anger, depression, addiction, anxiety, hopelessness, and debt. You can use it to invent a breakthrough technology, learn a new language, become a better parent or a stronger leader. Most important, you can use this idea with others—in your family, organization, team, industry, community, or the world—to create positive and significant change.

Individually and collectively, we're confronted by events and circumstances that can no longer be ignored. Political, social, environmental, and economic forces are upending life as we know it. Less than one-third of US employees are actively engaged at work, a trend that's continued for years. The dissatisfaction people feel right now is having serious global economic repercussions, which says nothing of the emotional, psychological, and spiritual costs straining our souls and society. An estimated 350 million people around the world suffer from depression, which is the leading cause of disability and a major contributor to the burden of disease. In the US, suicide rates are at a thirty-year high.

Every day we throw away more food in our homes, restaurants, and supermarkets than it would take to feed the nearly one billion people who go hungry.[1] As a species, we choose to spend more money each year on ice cream—a whopping $59 billion—rather than provide the basic human dignities of education, health care, and sanitation to all humans on earth, for a mere $28 billion.[2] We haven't even touched upon the systemic racism, corruption, pollution, violence, war inequality, and injustice that continue to cause pain across every corner of our planet.

Yet there can be no significant change in the world unless we first have the courage to change ourselves. In order to change ourselves, we must first believe we can.

Together, we'll use this one simple belief, *everything is figureoutable*, to activate our inherent ability to transform our lives and, by doing so, instigate meaningful change around us. Which is exactly why this book is in your hands right now.

We need you. We need your heart, your voice, your courage, your joy, your creativity, your compassion, your love, and your gifts. Now, more than ever.

2

Your Road Map to Results

You don't make progress by standing on the sidelines, whimpering and complaining. You make progress by implementing ideas.

Shirley Chisholm

J ust because this idea is simple doesn't mean the road ahead is easy. You'll need humility and courage. Self-compassion. A willingness to experiment. A sense of humor. And patience. Lots and lots of patience. As Carlos Castaneda shared, "We either make ourselves miserable, or we make ourselves strong. The amount of work is the same."

Before we continue on, the following road map ensures you get the most bang for your buck. Once mastered, the figureoutable philosophy will become a treasure you own in your heart, one that you can never lose.

1. TRAIN YOUR BRAIN
FOR GROWTH

Your brain is an extraordinary biocomputer, and it's constantly running programs that work either for or against you. That's why I want you to be aware of two destructive thoughts—viruses, if you will—that can pop up when you're learning something new. The trick is to catch these thought viruses and turn them into productive questions. Why? Because the brain is wired to answer questions. No matter what question you ask, your brain will immediately start searching for an answer. When you transform these thoughts into helpful, productive questions, you train your brain to help you learn, grow, and improve.

The first destructive thought to watch out for is "I know this already." Whenever we feel like we already know something, our minds disengage and shut down. The next time you hear yourself thinking or saying, "I know this already," especially as you read this book, immediately catch that thought and switch to a growth-minded question. Ask yourself, "What can I learn from this?" Ask it again and again with genuine curiosity. "What can I learn from this? *What* can I learn from this?"

You can always learn one of two things. First, you can learn a new angle to a concept you're familiar with. Or more likely, you'll realize that you're not fully executing on the thing you "already know." You're not living it. Knowing something intellectually is very different from doing something consistently, mastering it, and benefiting from it. Be humble. If you come across an idea or suggestion you've heard before, don't skim past it and say, "Whatever—I know this already." Be wiser than that. Ask the question *"What* can I learn from this?" and train your brain to find new opportunities for growth.

The second destructive thought virus is "This won't work for me." Instead of saying, "This won't work for me," which instantly shuts down the possibility of anything working, stop, catch it, and change it to a more productive question. Ask yourself, "How can this work me? *How can this work for me?*" Asking this question again and again forces you to look beyond the obvious, stretch outside your cognitive comfort zone, and poke holes in your own status quo. You'll train your brain to find new connections, innovations, opportunities, and possibilities that otherwise would have been missed.

Instead of . . .	Ask yourself . . .
"I know this already."	"*What* can I learn from this?"
"This won't work for me."	"*How* can this work for me?"

2. TRY IT BEFORE YOU DENY IT

Let's make one thing clear. I don't pretend to have all the answers. Nor does this book. But in these pages you'll get a simple framework and set of tools to help you find or create your own. If you're a person who thrives on playing devil's advocate, you might already be thinking, *No, Marie. Everything is NOT figureoutable. What about X, Y, or Z . . . ?*

Look, if you try hard enough, I'm sure you can conjure up something fantastical that's not technically figureoutable. Or not figureoutable—yet. For example, you can't bring your childhood dog back from the dead (though there are scientists working on cryogenics, and dog cloning *is* happening). You can't figure out how to grow working human wings out of your back (although we humans can indeed fly).

Sure, there's no scientific evidence to confirm my hypothesis that everything *is* actually figureoutable, but you'll never grow beyond your current circumstances if you're closed off to everything except what you currently know. Even if this entire book is bullshit, can you think of a more empowering and pragmatic philosophy to embrace? Can you imagine a more useful and supportive belief than *everything is figureoutable*?

With that in mind, here are three rules of play. This mental container helps you stay focused on what matters—your growth, your fulfillment, and your ability to access your inborn wisdom to solve problems and contribute to others.

Rule 1. All problems (or dreams) are figureoutable.

Rule 2. If a problem is not figureoutable, it's not really a problem—it's a fact of life or law of nature (e.g., death or gravity).

Rule 3. You may not care enough to figure this problem out or achieve this particular dream. That's okay. Find another problem or dream that ignites a blazing fire in your heart and go back to Rule 1.

As David Deutsch says, "Everything that is not forbidden by laws of nature is achievable, given the right knowledge." You don't need to take a quantum theorist's word for it. Or my word, for that matter. Instead, test it. Apply it. Experience it. Live it. See for yourself. If you're hellbent on looking for reasons why this won't work, congratulations. It won't. But neither will anything else.

3. DON'T OFFEND YOURSELF

Like sea salt crushed over a fresh caprese salad, you'll find swear words sprinkled throughout these pages. I write the way I speak, raw and from the heart.

My suggestion? Don't offend yourself. If you're going to clutch your pearls and gasp in horror seeing words like "clusterfuck" or "shitstorm" in print, let us lovingly part ways now. In a similar vein, I've chosen to keep the prose simple by using pronouns like "she" and "he." Please know that this book is for everyone, regardless of gender identity.

In the nearly two decades of my career, I've had the honor of helping people create meaningful change in their lives—people who come from a dazzling array of socioeconomic, ethnic, and cultural backgrounds. From ages six to eighty-six. People who are homeless. People with disabilities. People who are depressed and suicidal. People who have lost children, spouses, and loved ones. People recovering from horrific abuse and lifelong addiction, and people who are battling a terminal disease.

As a white woman born in the US, I'm well aware that I've won what Warren Buffett calls the Ovarian Lottery. That said, this book is filled with compelling, diverse stories far beyond my own. While not every anecdote, tool, or exercise will be a match for your situation, please don't use the "easy for you to say; you're so _____ [lucky, privileged, etc.]" argument to let yourself off the hook from exploring a concept that could be of value in your life. Remember to ask, "What can I learn from this? How can this work for me?"

I respect you. I respect and appreciate our differences. The fact that you picked up this book tells me that we share some DNA. We're both students and seekers.

While I don't know the details of your history or hardships, I do know this: Your innate power is immense. Your potential is limitless. You are unique, valuable, capable, and worthy of the dreams in your heart. Most of all, you have what it takes to transform and transcend whatever challenges you face.

4. DO THE WORK

Most books are designed to help you acquire new information. Some are made with the hope that you'll feel inspired. My intention goes far beyond that. **I'm committed to helping you get results.** For that to happen, you must do the work and complete the Insight to Action Challenges in this book with your full effort. I'm talking total, down-to-your-bones commitment. Because insight without action is worthless. Taking action is the only path to change.

Not every exercise will produce mind-blowing insights, but neither of us can predict which challenge will trigger a seismic paradigm shift or game-changing "aha." You'll get out of this what you put in. So don't *think* your answers to those that require writing. Don't say, "That sounds interesting, I should try it someday," to a challenge that says, "Do this now."

I also heartily recommend that you complete all written exercises by hand—in a journal or notebook—rather than on a keyboard, if possible. Studies show that writing notes by hand helps you learn, understand, and retain new information more effectively than typing. More than that though, writing by hand forces your brain to slow down and allows you to express your ideas and feelings more clearly and deeply. Putting pen to paper is a mystical way to access your most profound truths.

Do the work as suggested. Give your very best. If something doesn't make sense right now, earmark it and come back later. The point is to stay in action and keep moving forward. All it takes is one new perspective or tool, and your life will never be the same again.

You'll also notice that some of the key points circle back on themselves. Any repetition is by design. Repetition is a key principle in neuroplasticity. It's how we rewire our brains and turn good ideas into permanent new ways of being and behaving.

Like life, the figureoutable philosophy is a spiral path. Expect to hit some of the same issues again and again, each time at a different level. My goal is to help you master the fundamental mindsets and habits you need to figure anything out, for the rest of your life. You don't need to add 479 tasks to your morning routine or dozens of complex, time-consuming techniques. The figureoutable philosophy requires just a handful of tools and tenets that will alter the trajectory of your life. Simple is elegant and extremely efficient.

Nothing in this book will work unless you do. Experiment with the ideas, suggestions, and action challenges for at least thirty days. It's taken your entire lifetime to acquire and reinforce your current beliefs and behaviors, so there will naturally be some deprogramming required.

I'm confident that in one month of consistent, good-faith practice (and that's *daily good-faith practice*!) you'll see significant, noticeable improvements. More than enough to encourage you to keep going.

5. CONNECT WITH OUR COMMUNITY

The figureoutable philosophy becomes geometrically more powerful (and fun!) when applied in collaboration with others. You'll reach your collective goals faster and with a greater sense of joy, creativity, and camaraderie than ever before. That's why one of the greatest joys of my life is connecting with growth-minded, creative souls like you. As you operationalize the figureoutable philosophy, share your wins and break-throughs with me at MarieForleo.com/EIF. You'll also find a ton of additional free resources, hundreds of episodes of our award-winning show *MarieTV* and *The Marie Forleo Podcast* (guaranteed to get you out of any funk—fast), and one of the kindest and most supportive global communities on the planet.

As you're about to discover, *everything is figureoutable* is more than just a fun phrase to say. It's a practical, actionable discipline. A mantra that helps you operate at your best and achieve what you want. It's a mindset to help you solve meaningful problems, learn new skills, and find ways to help and contribute to others. Once adopted, this attitude will make you virtually unstoppable.

Not unstoppable in the sense that everything will always go your way, because it won't. And not unstoppable in that you'll never get disappointed, face rejection, suffer defeat, or find yourself in extraordinarily challenging situations, because you definitely will. But unstoppable in the most profound sense. Meaning that nothing—no thing, no person, no fear, no limitation, no circumstance—will ever again have the power to hold you back.

Let's roll.

Figureoutable Field Notes

She used everything is figureoutable *to help her mom get the care she needed in her last five weeks.*

A while back, I watched Marie's Oprah talk, "Everything Is Figureoutable." I loved it so much I shared it with my mum—it's a lesson I knew she'd been trying to teach me. She just loved it.

Then suddenly, everything changed. My beautiful mum was diagnosed with pancreatic cancer. Nothing seemed figureoutable. But you know what? When I looked deeper and stopped railing against what was happening, the little things were figureoutable.

Like trying to find nursing care for my mum, who lived in a rural area. Like finding special foods she could tolerate. Like getting medical equipment so she could spend her last days (and last five weeks) in her home. So I can honestly say, yes, everything is figureoutable. You've got to break the big things down into small bits so you can figure them out.

Thanks, Marie and team. You've made a difference to two people living on the other side of the world.

—JENN
NEW ZEALAND

3

The Magic of Belief

ALICE: This is impossible.
THE MAD HATTER: Only if you believe it is.
Alice in Wonderland (2010 film)

I felt like a total failure. Less than a year earlier, I'd graduated as the valedictorian of Seton Hall University. Yet here I was, sitting on the steps of Trinity Church in lower Manhattan, in tears.

Being the first in my family to get a college degree, I felt the weight of the pressure to make good on my education. As a trading assistant on the floor of the New York Stock Exchange on Wall Street, I had pride, a steady paycheck, and health insurance. I was grateful to have a job, but inside I felt like I was dying. To be clear, I gave it my all. I got to the office early, put on my game face, and worked my ass off to be the best trading assistant I could be.

But no matter how hard I tried, something just wasn't right. This little voice inside me kept whispering, *This isn't it. This isn't where you're supposed to be. This isn't what you're supposed to be doing with your life.*

More than 99.9 percent of the people I worked with were men, many of whom liked to hit the strip clubs and do a few lines of coke after the 4:00 p.m. closing bell. That wasn't my scene. What's more, the near daily propositions and sexual innuendo from my male colleagues was exhausting. At one point, I cut off my hair in protest, thinking a stark look would help me be taken more seriously. It didn't work, but I did my best to suck it up because I didn't know what else to do. I was confused because, on the surface, most of the guys I worked with had achieved the trappings of "traditional success." They had power and security, and were making millions. But on an emotional and spiritual level, many seemed bankrupt. They pined for their two priceless vacation weeks like they were the only thing they had to live for.

For a while, I tried to ignore that small voice inside. Tune it out. Focus on the task at hand. But the voice only grew louder. Then, one day, I was running tickets on the floor of the exchange and started to feel physically sick. I couldn't breathe. I told my boss I needed to head outside to grab a quick coffee. Instead, I made a beeline for the nearest church, which was near the intersection of Wall Street and Broadway. Being raised Catholic and having just graduated from a Catholic university, I was trained to ask God for help as my go-to fix in a crisis.

"What is WRONG with me?" I asked. "Am I going crazy here? Why can't I stop these voices in my head? If it's You telling me to quit, can You also please tell me what exactly I'm supposed to do instead?! It's not like I have a backup plan. Throw me a sign. I'm dying down here."

After a few minutes of pray-crying, I got my first clue on what to do next. *Call your dad.*

This made sense. The guilt of knowing how much he sacrificed to pay for my education was eating me alive. Now, I was having mild panic attacks because all I could think about was quitting, but I had no other job lined up and no other way to support myself.

I sat down on the church steps and opened my flip phone. (Remember those?) I barely got a full sentence out before I started bawling again.

"Dad, I'm SO sorry . . . I don't know what to do . . . I HATE where I work. I've tried everything I can think of, but nothing's helping. This doesn't make any sense—I'm grateful to have a job. I love working. I feel ashamed to even say this, but I keep hearing these voices in my head. They say I'm not supposed to be doing this. That I'm meant for something else. But they don't tell me what I'm supposed to be doing *instead* . . . I know how hard you and Mom worked to put me through school . . ."

I paused to wipe my face and catch my breath when my dad broke in. "Ree, calm down. You've always been a hard worker. You got a job at nine years old! You'll figure out a way to pay your bills. If you can't stand this job, leave. You're going to spend the next fifty years working hard. You have to find something you really love doing."

I had no idea how to find work I'd love doing. Even the idea of trying felt wildly irresponsible. And yet, I knew he was right. Within a week, I handed in my notice and embarked on a journey to discover what the hell I was meant to do in this world. To say I was full of fear was an understatement, but I was more invigorated than I'd ever been in my life.

The first thing I did was start bartending and waiting tables again so I could pay my rent. Then I applied to Parsons School of Design in NYC, because I was hunting for clues about what I would love to do for work. As a kid, I loved art, so I started there. But after I went through the application process and was admitted, I changed my mind. Turns out, going back to school didn't feel right either. What I did know was that I needed to be more creative at work. Searching for signs, I found a summer adult art program in Boston. I moved into an attic apartment above a Japanese art studio and continued to rack my brain for possible career paths. My only clues were that I loved people, I loved the world of business, and I was highly creative. Then I had an idea: Maybe I belonged in magazine publishing. It made sense. There's the business aspect of advertising and the creative realm of editorial. Maybe that's what I was supposed to do! So I returned to New York to give it a shot.

I hustled, went to temp agencies, and finally landed a job as an ad sales assistant at *Gourmet* magazine. The first few months were great. I loved learning about ad sales and getting to be part of a team that was producing a beautiful monthly product. My boss was smart and kind. Best of all, my desk was right next to the test kitchen, and the editorial staff would bring me samples. (Did I mention I love food?) Things seemed to be going well.

But after the novelty wore off and I began to understand what a future in this career would look like, I started hearing those same voices again. *This still isn't it, Marie. This isn't where you're supposed to be. You need to quit.*

NOOOOO! Not again! I was filled with shame and dread. What the hell was *wrong* with me? It made zero sense. I love working. I held multiple jobs throughout high school and college. Why couldn't I just be happy?

I tried to look more objectively at the situation, which is when I realized something interesting. I had no desire to one day become my boss (an ad executive), or my boss's boss (the publisher). I thought to myself, *If I don't want to climb this corporate ladder, what the heck am I doing wasting their time and mine?*

Maybe these past few jobs were focused too heavily on the business side of things. My past gigs centered on sales, money, and numbers. What about my creativity? Maybe publishing was the right industry, but I'd be happier on the editorial side instead. It was worth a shot. I leveraged my connections and secured a position as a fashion assistant in the editorial department of *Mademoiselle* magazine. *Okay, this has got to be it*, I thought. *I'll be working with highly creative people doing interesting things. Going to fashion shows, helping on photo shoots, designing layouts, seeing all of the newest collections and accessories. What's not to love?*

It was exciting at first. I loved meeting new people and learning the ins and outs of editorial production.

But then . . . it started again. Less than six months later, the inner voices came back, this time even stronger. *Wrong again. This still isn't you. This isn't where you're supposed to be or what you're supposed to be doing with your life.*

F U U U U U C K!!

A deep panic set in. I felt so embarrassed and confused and, frankly, damaged. I knew how lucky I was to have a job. But, at the same time, my body and heart revolted. Everything felt wrong. I scrambled to find some kind of reason. Was my brain broken? Did I have some type of cognitive or emotional or behavioral dysfunction? Was I just a loser with commitment issues who'd never amount to anything? Nothing made sense. How could I be the valedictorian of my graduating class, be an extremely hard and dedicated worker, and still be this clueless after a string of dream jobs? At that point, it had been a few years since I graduated. My friends were all getting promotions and building adult lives. All I wanted was to quit my job. Again.

Then one day at work, I stumbled across an article about a brand-new profession, "coaching." (This was the late 1990s—it was *all* so new back then.) Coaching was a burgeoning industry focused on helping people set and achieve goals, both personal and professional. One of the things that resonated with me was how coaching was distinct from psychotherapy. Therapy is about healing the past. Coaching is about creating your future. (Side note: I started off as a psych major in college but promptly walked out of my first class four minutes in when my Psych 101 professor started his lecture with "as you're about to discover, everything that's wrong with you can be traced back to your parents . . ."

Even as a seventeen-year-old, I knew blaming your parents for what's wrong in your life wasn't productive. I walked to the bursar's office and immediately switched my major to business administration.)

Not kidding. When I read that article about coaching, something inside me lit up. Clouds parted, choirs sang, and baby cherubs shot sunbeams out of their eyes, directly into my heart. A deep, gentle presence inside me said, *This is who you are. This is who you're meant to be.* Of course, my rational mind was quick to doubt.

Marie, you're twenty-frickin'-three years old. Who in their right mind is ever going to hire a twenty-three-year-old life coach?! You've barely lived life!! Not to mention you can't hold down a job. You're a mess. You're in massive debt. You have nothing to offer anyone. Who do you think you are!?! Are you nuts? This is the dumbest, stupidest thing I've ever heard. And can we please talk about how cheesy "life coach" sounds?

Despite the barrage of self-ridicule, I couldn't deny how right this felt in my bones. That persistent, stubborn inner knowing was like nothing else I'd ever experienced. No matter how hard I tried, I couldn't get this idea out of my head. Within a few days, I had enrolled in a three-year coach training program. I worked at *Mademoiselle* during the day and studied at night and on weekends.

About six months into my training, I got a call from the HR department at Condé Nast. They were offering me a promotion. At *Vogue*. It was more money and a lot more prestige. This was my fork in the road. Do I stick with the steady paycheck and health care, and work at the top fashion magazine in the world, or do I quit and start my own weird-ass coaching business? Cue the vicious fear ensemble erupting in my head . . .

Life coaching is the stupidest thing. Ever.
You have no clue how to start or run a business.

Who do you think you are!?!
This is insane.
You're a loser.
Everyone is going to laugh at you.
You're in debt up to your eyeballs.
You're a mess. You can't help anyone—who are you kidding?
Watch. This will be one more thing you'll fail at.

And yet, a calmer, preverbal presence practically pushed me out the corporate door. I turned down the *Vogue* gig and quit my job at *Mademoiselle*, too.

I spent the next seven years slowly (very, very, very slowly) building my business, all the while supporting myself through bartending, waiting tables, cleaning toilets, personal assisting, teaching fitness, dance— you name it. Nearly two decades later, I can say that the only thing that allowed me to take that leap was because a deeper, wiser part of me believed that somehow I'd be able to figure it out.

WHERE ARE YOU?

The ancestor of every action is a thought.
Ralph Waldo Emerson

Look around right now. No, really. *Do it.*

Wherever you are, whatever you're doing, stop reading and notice every item within your eyeshot. Become aware of what's in your hands (including this book), the devices you have near you, what you're wearing (if anything—*hello!*), what you're sitting in or standing on, and any and all objects or structures that surround you.

Here's what I see: My fingerprint-smudged laptop screen. A coffee mug. A wall of wooden kitchen cabinets covered in chicken wire and filled with glasses, vases, and books. A spiral-bound notebook. A few bottles of wine. That's just the obvious stuff.

There's a good chance we're both sitting amid a few modern miracles like electricity, indoor plumbing, and Wi-Fi. Do you realize that virtually everything that surrounds us was once *only* a thought? An idea? A wild, formless figment of someone's imagination?

Every movie you've ever seen. Every story you've ever heard. Every book you've read. Every song that's made you sing, dance, or cry has taken the mystical journey from the world of unmanifest to the manifest. From formless idea to concrete reality. These minds of ours are magical creation machines. They're the birthplace of every extraordinary experience we've ever encountered and every major breakthrough in human history. Our minds are what give us the power to manufacture reality, both for ourselves and others. That's because . . .

Everything in the material world is first created on the level of thought.

At six years old, I was walking in downtown New York City with my parents. Suddenly, a zinger of a thought popped into my young mind: *I'm going to live here one day.*

This idea was so unquestionable and exciting, I couldn't help but say it out loud. I stopped in the middle of the sidewalk near Bleecker and Perry Streets, held my hands in the air, and shouted, "I'm going to live here when I grow up!"

Puzzled, my mom said, "WHAT are you talking about?! We live in

New Jersey. That's where you go to school. That's where your friends are. That's where me and Daddy are and that's where you belong."

"No, Mom. I belong here. When I grow up, I'm going to live here and work here and have my very own apartment right here. You'll see!"

Took me seventeen years, but eventually I made that idea my reality. In fact, the West Village is the only neighborhood I've called home in the nearly twenty years I've lived in New York. Never more than a few short blocks from that original six-year-old's declaration.

I bet you've got an idea-to-reality story, too. A time where you had a mere thought about something you wanted to see, do, create, experience, or become—and you eventually did it.

Maybe it was a thought about your education, playing a sport or musical instrument, or having a particular career. Maybe it was an idea about something you wanted to make or develop. Maybe it was about traveling to a specific place, learning a skill, having a certain relationship, or starting a business. Maybe it was about healing an addiction or getting out of debt.

At first, that idea may have seemed like a long shot. You might have had no clue how to make it happen, or if it was even possible for you. But somehow you turned that idea into reality. That's a breathtaking power, isn't it? Sadly, it's one many of us take for granted, which is why it's so important that we remind ourselves . . .

Nothing exists in our world that does not first exist in our mind.

That's the universal gift we've been given to help us shape our lives and, collectively, the world around us. We're born creators with an innate power to bring our ideas and visions into reality. Though admittedly simplified, the process of creation goes something like this:

Thought → Feeling → Behavior → Result

While this might seem painfully obvious, this formula is one we can easily forget—especially as it relates to things we want to figure out.

Beneath our thoughts, however, lies an even deeper force that directs and controls our lives. It's a critical component of the creative process, both individually and collectively. In fact, this force *shapes* our thoughts and feelings. It dictates every aspect of our behavior: how much we sleep, what we choose to eat, what we say to ourselves and others, if and how much we exercise, and what we do with our time and energy. It helps birth our self-worth and our net worth. It impacts our health and fuels our feelings. It determines the quality of our relationships and, ultimately, whether we lead a life of joy, accomplishment, and contribution or one of misery, pain, and regret.

It's a force that underpins every action we take and how we interpret and respond to the world around us. This deeper, commanding force is our beliefs. **Beliefs are the hidden scripts that run our lives.**

Like a track running underneath a train, our beliefs determine where we go and how we get there. But before we start talking about concepts without clearly defining them, let's use this shared definition: A belief is something you know with total and absolute certainty. It's a thought that you've decided—consciously or unconsciously—is The Truth. Our beliefs are the root of our reality and our results.

Therefore, our creation formula looks more like this:

Belief → Thought → Feeling → Behavior → Result

In order to solve any problem or achieve any dream, we must first make a change at the level of belief. Because when you change a belief, you change everything.

THE HUMAN BODY ON BELIEF

Turns out, our beliefs control our physical body, too. In his excellent book *The Anatomy of Hope,* Jerome Groopman, MD, writes:

> Researchers are learning that a change in mindset has the power to alter neurochemistry. Belief and expectation—the key elements of hope—can block pain by releasing the brain's endorphins and enkephalins, mimicking the effect of morphine.

Intellectually, you know this. Let's say you're hiking in the woods. You catch a glimpse of something long, dark, and S-shaped on the path a few yards ahead. Immediately, your heart races, your palms sweat, and you tense up. "WTF!?!? Is that a *snake*?!?!" Your physiology shifts based on a nanosecond belief of possible danger ahead, even if that snake turns out to be a stick. This happens in more subtle ways, too. Who hasn't made a whopping headache *instantly* disappear when someone important calls and pulls our focus in a completely different direction? Or miraculously recovered from feeling sick or exhausted when an exciting "unmissable" invitation appears at the last minute?

I'm sure you've heard of the placebo effect. If not, it's the idea that if you believe something will help you feel better (like Advil), it will—even if you're just taking a sugar pill. But what about a placebo *surgery*?

Just wait until you hear this: Bruce Moseley, an orthopedic surgeon, was skeptical about the benefits of "arthroscopic surgery." So he tested it. He conducted a randomized, double-blind, placebo-controlled clinical trial, the gold standard in scientific research.

In the study, some of his patients would receive the full and complete knee surgery. Others would get a sham surgery, meaning they'd go through all the motions of real surgery (getting wheeled into the operating room, seeing the doctors in white coats, being put under anesthesia, etc.) but only receive a few shallow cuts to their knees and be sent home with a healing protocol and painkillers. One-third of the patients who received the real surgery experienced pain relief. But what stunned researchers was that one-third of patients who underwent the sham surgery had the same results. At one point during the study, those having the sham surgery enjoyed better results than those who got the real deal!

Here's another example. In 1962, the *Kyushu Journal of Medical Science* included a stunning report about an experiment focused on thirteen boys who were hypersensitive to the leaves of Japanese lacquer trees, which has poison-ivy-like effects. With their eyes closed, the thirteen boys were told that they were being touched on one arm with the poisonous Japanese lacquer leaves. Unsurprisingly, all thirteen boys had a dramatic skin reaction on their arms, including redness, itching, swelling, and blisters. The catch? Their arms were actually touched by the leaves of a harmless, nonpoisonous plant.

Then the researchers reversed the procedure. With their eyes still closed, the thirteen boys were told that they were being touched on their *other* arm by the leaves of a harmless plant. But in reality, those arms were now being touched by the poison-ivy-like leaves of the lacquer tree. This time, eleven of the thirteen boys showed *no* allergic skin reaction on their arms. None at all—despite the fact that they were highly sensitive to those rash-producing lacquer leaves.

Ultimately, the harmless leaves not only triggered a dramatic skin reaction but that reaction was greater than the one produced by the actual poisonous leaves. These intense physical responses simply come down to the monumental power of belief.[1]

Beliefs can also enhance our cognitive performance. In a small but insightful experiment, forty undergraduate students prepared to take a general knowledge test. Before doing so, half the students were told that just before each question, the correct answer would be momentarily and *subliminally* flashed on a screen in front of them. The authors of the study, Ulrich Weger and Stephen Loughnan, write, "We advised them that although they could no longer consciously recognize what was written, their unconscious would still be able to pick up the correct answer."

In truth, no correct answers were subliminally shown to that group of students. What they saw flash on the screen was a random string of letters. The result? Out of the two groups of students who took the general knowledge test, the group of students who were primed to believe they were subliminally shown the correct answers scored measurably higher on the test than the students who were not.[2]

Your beliefs are THE master commanders of your behavior and your results. Beliefs control our bodies and how we respond to crises, criticisms, and opportunities. They tell us what to notice, what to focus on, what it means, and what to do about it. The fact that your beliefs shape your reality is undeniable. They affect you physically, emotionally, spiritually, financially, intellectually, and culturally. Here's what's important to remember:

Long term, your beliefs determine your destiny.

Beliefs create behaviors. The cumulation of those behaviors adds up to your entire life.

Know what else? **Every belief has a consequence.** Your beliefs either heal you or harm you. They either support your aspirations or thwart them. Belief becomes the source of your limitation or your liberation. It doesn't matter what's true, it matters what you believe.

Because whatever you believe, you will react to. As clichéd as this Henry Ford quote has become, it's a fact: "Whether you think you can or you think you can't, you're right." Now does this mean that anyone can do or achieve anything they imagine as long as they believe hard enough? No, it does not. Consistent action, creativity, and commitment all play a role.

But one thing is certain. If you don't believe something is possible for you, it's not. Period. End of story. The moment you tell your brain, "That's not possible" or "I can't" or "That will never work for me," you're 100 percent right. You command your brain to shut down. The mind and body will follow.

While our potential as individuals is unknowable, what we know for sure is that limiting beliefs guarantees limited outcomes.

FROM "BORDERLINE RETARDED" TO COLLEGE GRADUATE

Test scores and measures of achievement tell you where a student is, but they don't tell you where a student could end up.

Carol Dweck

In the world of education, Marva Collins is a legend. Some consider her one of the greatest teachers of our time. Disillusioned after teaching in the public school system for sixteen years, Marva took $5,000 from her pension fund and opened the Westside Preparatory School in Chicago, Illinois, in 1975. Her goal was to open a school that would welcome students who'd been rejected by other schools, those labeled disruptive and essentially "unteachable." Her mission was to prove that all children can learn if given the proper attention, support, and instruction.

Marva's abilities were so impressive that she was asked by President Ronald Reagan to become secretary of education, but she declined so she could keep transforming one student at a time. An inspiring TV movie was made about her work starring Cicely Tyson and Morgan Freeman and, in 1994, Prince even featured Marva in his music video for "The Most Beautiful Girl in the World."

One student, named Erica, came to Marva when she was six years old and considered a hopeless case. Erica shared, "I was told that I was borderline retarded; that I would never read." Talk about a destructive and devastating belief! (By the same token, Thomas Edison's teachers said he was "too stupid to learn anything" and Albert Einstein didn't speak until he was four and couldn't read until he was seven.)

Yet Marva was undeterred. Erica began her studies at Westside Prep, and Marva imbued her with **an unquestionable belief** that she could, in fact, learn to read and write. This wasn't a hope or a wish from Marva; it was an irrefutable fact. Marva also instilled in Erica her trademark devotion to discipline, dignity, and relentless hard work.

When the CBS show *60 Minutes* profiled Marva and her students some sixteen years later, turns out that Erica did learn to read and write. So well, in fact, that she had just graduated from Norfolk State University.[3]

Take that in for a moment. Can you imagine how vastly different Erica's entire life would have been if she continued to believe the so-called experts who said she'd never read or write—that she was simply incapable of learning? Can you imagine the devastating ripple effect

EVERYTHING IS FIGUREOUTABLE

that belief would have had on Erica's family, emotionally and economically?

Now imagine the thousands of other students whose lives were forever transformed by adopting Marva's unshakeable belief. Think about the generations of families indelibly influenced by the power of one woman's conviction in a child's innate potential.

We begin to see just how tragic and cataclysmic limiting beliefs can be. Not only to our sense of self and ability to grow but also to the trajectory of our entire lives and our ability to contribute meaningfully to society. That's because . . .

When you change a belief, you change everything.

Our beliefs either propel us to or prevent us from living to our fullest potential. Our beliefs determine whether we fail or succeed, and how we define success in the first place. Just imagine the decades of relentless belief, action, and determination required to give women in the US the right to vote.

Or the unshakable belief that President John F. Kennedy and the team at NASA had in our ability to send humans into space and *walk on the moon*—something a mere one hundred years prior would have seemed preposterous.

Belief is where it all begins. It's the genesis of every remarkable discovery and leap forward humans have ever made from science to sports to business to technology and the arts.

The power that beliefs have over our lives simply cannot be overstated. But before we begin to change our beliefs, it's helpful to understand more about where they come from in the first place.

WHERE DO YOUR BELIEFS COME FROM?

She was crying uncontrollably. She hung up the phone and bent down so her eyes were even with mine. She grabbed my shoulders, shook me, and said, "Don't ever, ever, EVER let a man control your life, Marie. You need to make your own money. You need to CONTROL your own money. Don't be stupid like me. Don't make the same mistakes I've made. Do you hear me?! Do you see what's happening to me right now? After all these years, I have nothing. Nothing . . ."

That's what my mom said to me the day she and my father signed their divorce papers. I was eight. Once she let go, she put her head in her hands and sobbed. I stood there, frozen and terrified in our kitchen. I didn't know how to make things better or when I would see my dad again.

Everything felt unstable and unsafe.

Why is my mom crying? How can I make things better and get my dad back? What can I do to make sure that something like this never happens again?

One thing was clear: I knew my parents weren't fighting about drugs or alcohol or gambling. It was about money. Always money. Specifically, my mom having no control over it and, more broadly, that there was never enough to go around.

All I wanted was a way to get my family back together. Unwittingly, a powerful set of beliefs about money, men, and how the world worked began to take shape within me. Those beliefs sounded like this:

Not enough money = massive stress, pain, and suffering
Not enough money = losing love, security, connection,
    and family

Giving a man control over your money = being stupid and
   powerless
Giving anyone control over your life = ultimate regret and
   distress

Obviously, those beliefs aren't *the* truth, but as an eight-year-old,
they were ideas that I had decided were significant and true. I came to
those conclusions by listening to what I heard from adults and from
absorbing the emotions and circumstances I found myself in.

Some of our most pivotal beliefs are forged during significant emotional experiences—many of which happen in childhood. The more
heightened and penetrating the emotions, the more likely it is that they'll
shape our lives.

While standing in the kitchen with my mom, I made myself the deepest promise I'd ever made. Somehow, someday, I'd figure out a way to
make so much money that the lack of it would never take love away again.
The stress and instability caused by the scarcity of money was intolerable,
so my goal was to have an abundance of it. Not to buy toys or material
things, but as a vehicle to restore love and alleviate suffering. I remember
always seeing those classic "a dollar a day" ads on TV about children and
animals in need. Every commercial said that "just a little bit of money"
could help make a difference. I formed the *belief* that if I could earn a lot
of money, I'd not only help my own family, but other people, too.

Looking back, it's easy to see how some of those early beliefs like
"money is scarce" and there's "never enough to go around" played a part
in why I had trouble with money as a young adult. I went into debt and
struggled with my worth and earning capacity for years.

However, I never lost touch with that promise I made to one day figure money out and make enough to share. At a certain point in my early

twenties—once I was fed up with being broke—I became obsessed with reshaping my financial beliefs and behavior. I educated myself on personal finance, cleared out my negative money beliefs, and built strong financial habits that I'm grateful for to this day.

Here's what's useful about investigating our old beliefs. It's not an all-or-nothing game. We don't have to reject everything we believe wholesale. There may be some beliefs (or perhaps pieces of them) that are useful and worth keeping, but we won't know until we question them and see. So how does this intricate web of beliefs get established in the first place? Let's take a short tour.

1. ENVIRONMENT

When you arrived in this world, your baby brain was neutral and free. It contained no programming—no opinions, knowledge, biases, or beliefs. Then, like a sponge, you began to absorb ideas about yourself and others from your family, friends, caretakers, school, culture, and society. Just as we learn how to walk and talk, we learn what to believe. Little by little, our environment programs our brains with beliefs about everything from love, health, sex, work, our bodies, money, religion, beauty, relationships, other people, the world at large—you name it! Most important, our environment programs our brains with beliefs about our own capabilities.

Here's where things get dicey. Many of our most deeply held convictions are hand-me-downs. They're old, unexamined, and unquestioned ideas that we innocently accepted from others. We didn't take the time to examine, question, and *choose* them for ourselves. Sadly, many of those hand-me-down beliefs are counterproductive to what we're trying to achieve.

To be clear, when it comes to those hand-me-down beliefs, our parents, teachers, and caretakers did the best they could. Everyone is always doing the best they can. Blame and resentment have no place here. But it's important to recognize that, whether positive or negative, our environment is one of the most significant sources of our current beliefs. This was true for us as young children and it continues to be true for us as adults. That's why it's important to stay mindful of your environment, especially as you work to incorporate new, more supportive and expansive beliefs.

2. EXPERIENCE

Direct experience helps us further cement our beliefs about ourselves, others, and the world at large. Naturally, these beliefs are often influenced by hand-me-down beliefs.

Here's a simple example. I love roller coasters. It's hard for me to express how much joy and aliveness I feel when I'm on a fast, smooth, speeding bullet of a ride. It's something I first learned to enjoy with my dad. But I know lots of people who won't step foot near a roller coaster! In their experience, roller coasters mean terror, anxiety, and hours of motion sickness.

Direct experiences, both positive and negative, stack up over time and begin to coalesce into stronger and more deeply rooted beliefs about our identity, who we are, and what makes up our reality.

3. EVIDENCE

Evidence-based beliefs are thoughts and ideologies we accept as "the truth" from authoritative figures and sources: scientists, clergy, research studies, doctors, academics, authors, the media, and general society. But as technology, science, and culture progress, so does what we believe to be true. As such, our evidence-based beliefs can and do evolve over time. This is great news because it demonstrates that, as individuals and as a society, we can indeed change and evolve our beliefs. Remember— humans once believed the world was flat, that margarine was better than butter, and that an ice-pick lobotomy cured mental illness. Aren't you glad those days are over?

4. EXAMPLES

When Oprah Winfrey was sixteen, she saw Barbara Walters on television. She was so deeply moved and inspired that she said to herself, "Maybe I could do that." Oprah went on to share, "There's no other woman that deserves more in terms of opening the door for my career."[4] In that statement, Oprah is not talking about Barbara Walters "opening doors" by recommending her for broadcasting jobs. She's talking about the fact that merely *witnessing* another woman on television cracked open a possibility within Oprah's consciousness about what was possible for her. It's hard to become what you don't see.

Finding role models outside your immediate circle is one of the best and most powerful ways to transcend your own limiting beliefs. Alive or dead, famous or unknown, find inspiring examples through reading biographies, watching movies, listening to interviews, or simply paying closer attention to good people in your life.

5. ENVISIONING

Sometimes we have no examples to look to for inspiration, yet a belief in what's possible burns so brightly in our hearts that we devote our lives to making it a reality. Roger Bannister breaking the four-minute mile in 1954 is one example. No one had achieved this goal, yet deep in his heart he believed he could. So he did. Then countless others followed.

Dr. Martin Luther King Jr. described a vision of freedom and equality that didn't exist yet. In his iconic "I Have a Dream" speech, he shared:

> I have a dream that my four little children will one day live in a nation where they will not be judged by the color of their skin but by the content of their character.

Dr. King forever shifted our culture, and millions of people to this day are working toward his dream. Envisioned beliefs seem to emerge from another plane of consciousness—our intuition, or from some inner voice or vision—and get forged in the fire of our hearts.

WHY OUR BELIEFS
TEND TO STICK

We do not see things as they are, we see them as we are.
Anaïs Nin

Naturally, all five sources intertwine, overlap, and interact. They also tend to reinforce each other, which can create some hiccups when it comes to upgrading our beliefs if we don't keep a watchful eye.

For instance, perhaps as a result of your parents' divorce, you formed a belief that marriages never last. Then you personally went through a divorce that further cemented the belief. "See! Marriage just isn't worth the trouble." It's not hard to find even more evidence that reinforces those beliefs as the "truth." A quick search of popular statistics shows:

- Between 40 and 50 percent of first marriages end in divorce[5]
- In the US that means one divorce approximately every thirty-six seconds[6]
- That's nearly 2,400 divorces per day—16,800 divorces per week or 876,000 divorces a year!

Chances are, you'll continue to affirm the belief that "marriages never last" by listening for and retelling stories of broken marriages from family, friends, and the media.

This highlights another fundamental fact about our beliefs. **Our brains tend to reinforce what we already believe.** This well-documented phenomenon is called confirmation bias. Simply put, confirmation bias means we look for and find evidence to support our beliefs. We cherry-pick information that confirms what we already know, while ignoring (consciously and unconsciously) information that challenges our existing beliefs.

In this scenario, any example you find of a couple who's happily married either is immediately dismissed as a fluke or a lie, or doesn't even register on your mental radar because it doesn't line up with your existing belief!

Confirmation bias runs deep. Real deep. It's particularly pronounced as it relates to religion and politics, as well as our own self-identity. Which helps us understand why social, political, and personal discussions about topics like women's reproductive rights, climate change, immigration, race, and gun control can quickly devolve into screaming matches.

Having taken part in these kinds of "debates" with my family, I know that it rarely turns out well. Confirmation bias kicks in and all hell breaks loose. In my world, that means a lot of oversized hand gestures and four-letter words. Though we eventually wind up laughing and changing the subject, it's also true that we sometimes hunker down even harder in our own belief bunkers.

Although we can't eliminate confirmation bias altogether, awareness helps. By understanding that our minds are designed to reinforce that which we already believe (while automatically deleting anything to the contrary), we can do our best to stay open-minded. In doing so, we take another step toward mastering our minds rather than being mastered by them. The most important fact for you to remember is this:

All beliefs are a choice and choices can be changed.

That's right. Your beliefs are a *choice*. Every single one of them.

Since all beliefs are learned—either consciously or unconsciously—the ones that create pain, misery, and suffering can be unlearned.

Released.

Let go.

Any limiting belief can be erased and replaced. Best of all, changing your beliefs doesn't have to be hard, it just takes awareness, desire, and practice.

When you look more closely, a belief is nothing more than a *thought* that you've decided is significant and true. That's it! There's nothing actually holding that belief in place. No steel bars. No padlocks. No chains. Like any other thought that appears in your mind, you can deliberately choose to dismiss it.

You already have what it takes to transform yourself from a passive onlooker to a powerful creator of your destiny. So if you're unhappy with any of the beliefs you've chosen (or unconsciously accepted from others), choose again.

And again.

And again.

And again.

The first step to becoming free from your beliefs is noticing which ones are creating hurt or misery for you. Practice becoming aware of what you're thinking (i.e., believing) and know that, at any moment, you get to decide if you want to continue believing that thought.

Research has proven that our brains are highly adaptable. The brain is like a muscle in that it changes and gets stronger with use. Scientists often refer to this as "plasticity." Studies in neuroscience show that we can grow new neural networks and train our brain to think in new ways. Whatever thoughts we repeat most often and with the most emotional intensity, we reinforce. Physically, we strengthen and build those neural networks. That means we can literally hardwire beliefs into our brains and nervous systems. Whatever thoughts we don't use or reinforce will grow weak and eventually fade away.

Yes, permanently changing your neural pathways requires focus, repetition, and dedication. But seriously—can you think of a better use of your time than physically rewiring your brain to help you lead a better life?! Once you establish and reinforce new beliefs, those new ways of behaving will become habitual. That means better results with less conscious effort.

Naturally, our goal is to bolster the beliefs that support us and eliminate those that don't. But here's what's thrilling. There's no need to play Sherlock Holmes and hunt down every limiting belief rattling around in your mind. Instead, we'll take a smarter time-saving approach.

All you need is one core meta belief, a master key that unlocks every imaginable door in the castle of your consciousness. It's like throwing a switch that instantly illuminates a field of infinite potential. If you haven't yet guessed, the whole purpose of this book is to inspire you to adopt the supremely powerful belief that *everything is figureoutable*!

Like toppling the first domino, this one belief sparks a cognitive chain reaction that expands all other possibilities. Once you embrace this belief both functionally and operationally—not just conceptually—there is nothing in this world that can ever stop you again.

Let's start rewiring that beautiful brain of yours right now.

(Remember, repetition is a key principle of neuroplasticity.)

Say the following out loud. Even and especially if it feels silly.

Everything Is Figureoutable

Good.

Now say it out loud *again*. At least five more times. Each time, say it with increased energy, passion, and yes—gusto!

Everything Is Figureoutable

Everything Is Figureoutable

Everything Is Figureoutable

Everything Is Figureoutable

Everything Is Figureoutable!!

You're damn right it is.

Make yourself a promise. Say this phrase—both aloud and in your own head—as often as you can. Five, ten, fifty times a day. Make it a ritual. Why? Because . . .

The most powerful words in the universe are the words you say to yourself.

With enough energy and repetition, you'll plant this belief so firmly that it will awaken your consciousness on a deeper level.

Say "Everything is figureoutable" when you wake up in the morning. Sing it in the shower. Write it in your journal. Chant it while you're working out. (The more you can use your body and your emotions, the deeper this belief will root into your being.) Say it whenever you find yourself tossing and turning at night. The more you think it, say it, write it, and feel it in your body, the more you'll reinforce those neural tracks in your mind.

Soon, you'll begin to live with an expanded sense of creativity, confidence, and authority. Before you know it, *everything is figureoutable* will not only become your most treasured belief, but the cornerstone of your reality.

INSIGHT TO ACTION
CHALLENGE

If I didn't believe the answer could be found, I wouldn't be working on it.

Dr. Florence Sabin

Grab a journal and write your answers to the following questions. Remember, you won't get results by silently thinking these answers in your head. Put pen to paper. Anything less is half steppin'.

1. ***Why did you pick up this book?*** What is it that you want to solve, change, or figure out? You might have a laundry list—that's fine. Get it all out. Then choose the most important change you want to make now. (If you're not sure which is most important, we cover that in chapter 6. You can revise it then.)

2. ***What negative or limiting belief(s) have stopped you from figuring this out until now?*** What have you told yourself about you, your capabilities, others, the world, or reality that's prevented you from making this change once and for all?

3. ***Now, cross out each of those negative or limiting beliefs and write "BULLSHIT" next to each negative or limiting belief.*** (Do it. It's fun!)

4. *Next, riff on why each of those negative beliefs or stories are indeed total bullshit.* Litigate the other side. Make your best, most impassioned case for the exact opposite perspective. (Hint: A deeper, wiser part of you *already* knows those limiting beliefs are bullshit—otherwise you wouldn't have picked up this book.) Get real. Be honest. Answer from your heart, not your head.

5. *Now imagine, who would you be without this limiting belief?* What would be different in your life if you were *incapable* of ever thinking that negative, small-minded belief again? How might you behave differently in your relationships or at work? What might change for you physically, emotionally, mentally, financially, or spiritually? Really *imagine* yourself without this belief and describe your reality from that place.

6. *Design a creative, playful plan to embody the belief that* everything is figureoutable. Remember, repetition and emotion are key! Maybe you want to write the phrase twenty times in your journal every morning for the next ninety days. You could make "Everything Is Figureoutable" the wallpaper on your smartphone. Perhaps you'll chant it while washing dishes or folding laundry, or grunt it out loud while you're doing squats. Use as many modalities as you can—your voice, writing, graphics, audio, embodied movement, and most important, repetition. For more ideas and resources, visit Marie Forleo.com/EIF.

Figureoutable Field Notes

Movement is her life—but after this surgery, she'll never be able to move like that again.

My daughter is a competitive solo dancer and team hip-hop dancer. Movement is her life. She wore a body brace for scoliosis for twenty hours per day for three years and it didn't work. She eventually needed to get a spinal fusion surgery that fused eleven vertebrae, making it impossible for her to dance again.

For the last couple of years, I've been unable to accept this limitation her beautiful free body will have for the rest of her life. One night as I was lying in bed crying, yet again, I was scrolling through my phone and came across Marie's Oprah talk. It all clicked. I thought to myself, "What would Marie do in this situation? What would her mom do?" Then it came to me. "Damn, we'll figure it out!!"

So I did. It started with acceptance. I thought about what I wanted for my daughter's life overall: for her to be happy. Could she have a happy life with a broomstick in her back? Damn straight she could! My mission was to make it all beautiful. And it is. Emma has become a scoliosis icon and a model for the cause.

I worked backward toward the goal I wanted to achieve (a beautiful life for my daughter) versus focusing on what I thought would give her a beautiful life (dancing). My daughter is better off than before her diagnosis—mentally and physically—and I am at peace. I don't cry myself to sleep anymore.

I had a cool funky coffee cup made by an artist that says, "What would Marie's mom say?" and use it every day to remind me of this mantra. I came to believe that everything we need to know in the world is held within that one sentence, "Everything is figure-outable." Because it truly is.

—TARINA
MONTREAL

4

Eliminate Excuses

The worst lies are the lies we tell ourselves.
Richard Bach

Don't feel sorry for yourself. Only assholes do that.
Haruki Murakami

ver had a morning like this? You went to bed with every
intention of getting up early. You were going to work out,
meditate, write—you know, finally become that incredibly
productive human you know you can be. Now the phone is vibrating
next to your head. *Already? Noooo! It's so dark. I'm so cozy. Sleep is important
for my health, right? Just five more minutes.* Five minutes pass. *Okay, maybe ten
more.* By the time your feet hit the floor, you're chasing the day. The dog
is begging to be walked. Your phone is blowing up from an unexpected
meltdown at work. You notice a stain on your shirt after you've walked
out the door. Cue David Byrne: Same as it ever was, same as it ever was.

Now what about a morning like this? Your eyes pop open in the dark.

You turn your head and grab the phone. *Really, only 4:30 a.m.?* The alarm isn't set to go off for another hour. Your flight doesn't leave until 8:45 a.m., but you're so pumped for this trip that you can't sleep another minute. You hop out of bed, work out, and head off to the airport—early.

What's the deal? How is it that sometimes we're able to effortlessly get ourselves to do exactly what we need to do, but other times it's a struggle? What holds us back from consistently performing at the levels we're capable of?

To find the answer, we have to look inside. No matter what we're trying to figure out, the biggest barriers are often in our own minds:

> *I need to start exercising again, but I'm just so busy with work and the*
> *kids. Can't do it—no time.*
> *My finances are a mess. No matter what I do, I can't seem to get ahead.*
> *I'm just not a numbers person.*
> *I really want to take that design class. It could open up a whole new career!*
> *But it's too expensive—I can't afford it.*
> *I wish I could meet someone special. But I don't have time for dating, I'm*
> *too old, and besides, all the good ones are already taken.*

Sound familiar? My hand is raised because I've said things like this to myself. Many times. But here's the truth: One of the biggest obstacles that holds us back are those excuses. The little lies we tell ourselves that limit who we are and what we ultimately accomplish.

Everybody makes excuses from time to time, so don't feel bad. But if you're committed to figuring things out, all excuses have got to go. It's time to call yourself out and uncover all the ways you bullshit yourself. Once you get honest about how flimsy your excuses really are, you'll reclaim not only enormous stores of energy, but also your power to change.

TWO FOUR-LETTER WORDS THAT WILL ANNIHILATE YOUR BS EXCUSES

Let's start by looking at your language and two common words that blur your ability to be honest with yourself. Those two four-letter words are "can't" and "won't." Think about how often people say some version of the following:

I can't get up and work out every day.

I can't find the time to get writing done.

I can't forgive her for what she's done.

I can't take that job, it's across the country.

I can't ask for help.

I can't ask for a promotion because I'm not good enough yet.

I can't launch this project because my boss didn't approve it.

I can't _____ [take the class/learn the language/start the venture/ etc.] because I can't afford it.

Here's the problem: 99 percent of the time when we say we "can't" do something, "can't" is a euphemism for "won't." What does "won't" mean? "Won't" means we're not willing. In other words . . .

You don't really want to.

You don't want to do the work.

You don't want to take the risk.

You don't want to get uncomfortable or be inconvenienced. It's simply not a big enough or important enough priority.

Before you disagree or find exceptions (which there are), humor me for a moment.

If you consider how this might be true in your life, even a portion of the time, you'll break free from the vast majority of self-deceptive crap that holds you back. For example, go back to all those statements and replace "can't" with "won't." You'll discover something much more honest:

I won't get up and work out every day.
I won't find the time to get writing done.
I won't forgive her for what she's done.
I won't take that job, it's across the country.
I won't ask for help.
I won't ask for the promotion because I'm not good enough yet.
I won't launch this project because my boss didn't approve it.
I won't _____ [take the class/learn the language/start the venture,
etc.] because I won't afford it.

In my life, whenever I say "I can't," most of the time what I really mean is "I won't." I don't want to. I have no desire to make the sacrifice or put in the effort to get that particular result. It's not something I want badly enough or something I want to put ahead of my other priorities. Saying that you don't want something (or don't want to put in the work or sacrifice to get it) doesn't make you bad or lazy. It makes you honest.

Here's why this distinction is important, especially when it comes to leveraging the figureoutable philosophy. Often, when we use the word "can't," we start to behave like victims—powerless against our circumstances. It's as though we have no control over our time, energy, or choices. We take no responsibility for our lives.

When you use the word "won't," you feel and behave more powerfully. You remember that you're in charge of your thoughts and actions. YOU get to determine how to spend your time and resources. You'll feel more alive and energized and free because you're taking full responsibility for the state of your life.

Speaking of taking responsibility, a quick reminder about an essential universal principle:

You are 100 percent responsible for your life.

Always and in all ways. It's not your parents. It's not the economy. It's not your husband or your wife or your family. It's not your boss. It's not the schools you went to. It's not the government or society or institutions or your age. You are responsible for what you believe, how you feel, and how you behave. To be clear, I'm not saying you're responsible for the actions of others or injustices that have happened to you—but you are responsible for how you respond to the actions of others. In fact, lasting happiness can *only* come when you take 100 percent responsibility for yourself.

Now you might say, "Marie, you don't know my story. So many horrific things have happened to me that aren't my fault, that are outside my control, and that I didn't choose. How can I be responsible for that?" Or you might say, "But, Marie, things are happening to me right now that I have no control over because of the culture and society I was born into. How am I responsible for those things?"

You're right. There are external forces, situations, and social constructs that affect us all. What's crucial to understand is that no matter what happened in your past or what's happening now, if you're not at least *willing* to take full responsibility for your life—which includes your thoughts, feelings, and behavior—you give up the power to change it.

Tiffany, a psychotherapist in San Francisco, wrote to me and said:

> It's easy for those of us who come from modest backgrounds or have generational histories of social trauma and disenfranchisement to be bogged down by the weight of despair. As the daughter of my once-impoverished African American dad, I inherited the hopelessness that comes from a legacy of being beaten down, having rights removed, fighting and then having one's land, home, family wrenched away no matter what you do. In tiny ways, that mentality would defeat my efforts. I'd start something, come upon an obstacle, and grow sad, not realizing that I could figure it out. I DO have the resources to make something happen. Marie, you taught me this! As someone who has struggled for YEARS with how to move forward and then do it, one thing you said changed my life. EVERYTHING IS FIGUREOUTABLE.

To be clear, taking responsibility doesn't mean staying silent about injustice. It doesn't mean blaming or shaming yourself. It doesn't mean beating yourself up or living with constant guilt. Instead, taking 100 percent responsibility for your life means recognizing that you're in charge of deciding how you feel and who you wish to be *in response* to what happens now and in the future.

Could you imagine if Malala Yousafzai felt she wasn't old enough, privileged enough, or strong enough to champion girls' education? Remember, Malala was a *preteen* at just eleven years old when she began to fight for girls' rights to go to school. She was only fifteen when she was shot in the head by the Pakistani Taliban during an assassination attempt. Remarkably, she survived and addressed the United Nations on her sixteenth birthday. At seventeen, she was the youngest person to ever receive the Nobel Peace Prize. Malala refused to allow a bullet to the head to become an excuse to stop advocating for education.

> The best years of your life are the ones in which you decide your problems are your own. You do not blame them on your mother, the economy, or the president. You realize that you control your own destiny.
>
> *Albert Ellis*

Do you know the story of Bethany Hamilton? When she was thirteen, this aspiring athlete went for a morning surf with friends at Tunnels Beach, Kauai. She was lying on her board with her arm dangling in the sea when a fourteen-foot tiger shark attacked, severing her entire left arm below the shoulder. By the time she arrived at the hospital, Bethany had lost 60 percent of her blood and was in hypovolemic shock. It was unclear whether she'd survive.

Bethany pulled through and, despite her extraordinary trauma, was determined to get back in the water. One month after the shark attack, she returned to the sea and her surfboard. A little over a year later, she won her first national surfing title and has gone on to win and place in many more events, competing regularly and fulfilling her lifelong dream of being a professional surfer.

After that harrowing event, it would have been completely understandable for Bethany to say some version of "I can't" and decide that losing her arm meant the end of her surfing career instead of the beginning.

In her darkest hour, Bethany made an important choice. She chose to take responsibility for herself and her future. She chose to meet her circumstances with grace, courage, and determination. She decided that this life-altering event wouldn't stop her from pursuing her dreams. In fact, it would do the opposite—it would fuel her to work even harder. She made no excuses and figured it out. In doing so, she's become an awe-inspiring model of the indomitable strength of the human spirit.[1]

Here's one more example. In rural Zimbabwe, an eleven-year-old girl named Tererai was in primary school for less than a year before her father married her off, for the price of a cow, to a man who would beat her regularly. She desperately wanted an education, but she was poor and a girl. Using her brother's schoolbooks and leaves as paper, Tererai taught herself to read and write. Still, by the time she was eighteen she was the mother of four.

Years later, Tererai met an international aid worker who asked every woman in her village about their greatest dreams. Inspired, Tererai wrote her wildest dreams on a scrap of paper. She hoped to one day study abroad, earn a bachelor's degree, a master's, and then a doctorate.

Her mother looked at those dreams and said, "Tererai, I see you only have four dreams, personal dreams, but I want you to remember this. Your dreams in this life will have greater meaning when they are tied to the betterment of your community." And so Tererai wrote down a fifth dream: "When I come back I want to improve the lives of women and girls in my community, so they don't have to go through what I had gone through in my life."[2]

Given her circumstances, those were pretty far-reaching goals. Some might even say impossible. Tererai sealed those dreams in a tin box and buried them under a rock.

Tererai began working with local aid organizations as a community organizer. She saved every penny she could and used some of her earnings to take correspondence courses to quench her thirst for education. In 1998, she applied and was accepted to Oklahoma State University. With the support of the organizations she worked for and her community, she made her way to the US to study—with her now five children in tow, husband, and $4,000 in cash wrapped around her waist.

Despite this breakthrough, Tererai's life became harder than ever. Her family lived in a tattered trailer. Her kids were constantly hungry and cold. Instead of helping out, her husband continued to beat her. Tererai fed herself and her children from trash cans. She considered giving up, but found the strength to press on because she believed quitting would somehow let down other African women. As recalled in the excellent book by Nicholas Kristof and Sheryl WuDunn called *Half the Sky*, Tererai said, "I knew that I was getting an opportunity that other women were dying to get."[3]

Tererai worked tirelessly at multiple jobs and attended class as best she could, enduring little sleep and sustained abuse from her husband. At one point, she was nearly expelled from school because she was late on her tuition payments. Miraculously, a university official stepped in to advocate on her behalf and rally support from the local community.

Tererai finally got her violent husband deported and continued to persevere. She earned both her BA and her MA. Every time she achieved a goal, she returned to Zimbabwe, dug up that piece of paper, and checked off another box. Tererai remarried a plant pathologist named Mark Trent and continued pushing ahead. Eventually, in 2009 she was able to check off the final goal on her list: completing her doctoral dissertation, receiving her PhD, and at long last, becoming forever known as Dr. Tererai Trent.

Today, she is the founder of Tererai Trent International, an organization whose mission is to provide universal access to quality education while also empowering rural communities. Want to know what Tererai's favorite life motto is? "*Tinogona*," meaning "It is achievable!"

I couldn't agree more.

Can you imagine all the excuses Tererai could have used to hold herself back or quit? Pretty valid excuses at that. While her journey wasn't easy or fast, Dr. Trent proves once again the possibilities that await us when we focus on the results we want rather than reasons why we can't (or won't).

If these folks didn't let excuses—or anything else—hold them back from figuring out their dreams, why should we? This reminds me of one of my favorite quotes. "Life is 10 percent what happens to me and 90 percent how I react to it." It's part of a longer passage, which reads:

> Attitude is more important than facts. It is more important than the past, than education, money, circumstances, than failures and success, than what other people think, say, or do. It is more important than appearance, ability, or skill. It will make or break a business, a home, a friendship, an organization. The remarkable thing is I have a choice every day of what my attitude will be. I cannot change my past. I cannot change the actions of others. I cannot change the inevitable. The only thing I can change is attitude. Life is 10 percent what happens to me and 90 percent how I react to it.[4]

You always have more power than you think. Your mind is the most extraordinary tool you have to shape your reality.

Let me ask you this: Isn't it true that at some point in your life—when you really, *really* wanted something, when it was supremely important to you—you somehow figured out a way to make it happen? An inner switch flipped and, suddenly, you got resourceful. You got committed. You created results despite the odds.

Scan the mental Rolodex of your past. What's one instance where, at first, you believed you didn't have the time, ability, or resources to make something happen—and yet, you figured it out anyway? Here are a few simple examples from my own life.

In college, I was a dedicated student and held down multiple jobs. Nine times out of ten, when friends invited me to parties or concerts, my response would be, "Thanks, but I can't go because I've got work to do." From my perspective, it wasn't a lie or an excuse. That's what I believed to be true.

There was one particular night where I had both an important ethics exam to study for and a law brief to finish. My intention, as usual, was to stay in and work. But before I made it back to my dorm, I ran into a guy I liked. He asked me to go to an event that night. Rather than my reflexive, "No, I can't—I don't have time," something made me pause (hello, hormones!), and instead I said, "Sounds great. See you at seven."

I still had every intention of getting my work done, but that extra motivation made me realize it wasn't about having the time, it was about *making* the time. And there's always more time than we realize (more on that later).

I got hyperfocused, stayed up late, and woke up early the next morning to fit it all in, without cutting corners on my studies. The desire to both excel in class and go on that date helped me push beyond my comfort zone and far beyond my well-worn "I don't have time" excuse. The time was there. I just had to want it bad enough.

Early in my career, I learned about a retreat in South America that I really wanted to go on. The problem was that I didn't have the money. I was still deep in debt and working constantly to pay it off. This scenario had happened before; I'd come across other educational events that were intriguing, but I'd tell myself, *Maybe someday, but right now I can't afford it.* That was usually the end of the discussion.

There was something different about this particular trip. Logically, I couldn't explain it. I just felt this persistent pull in my body. I knew in my heart that somehow I had to be there. Have you ever had that experience? Where you know something deep down that defies logic and reason? Whether you call it gut instinct or intuition, it's wise to listen.

Unable to shake the feeling that I *had* to go on this trip, I made a bold move and negotiated a special payment plan with the retreat organizers. I gave them my word that no matter what it took or how long it might take, I would not let them down on my financial commitment. Then I hustled my ass off. I found three extra side jobs to make it happen.

That was back in 2003 and it's still one of the most profound experiences of my life. Turns out, that trip was where Josh, my beloved partner, and I fell in love. Looking back, I'm thankful not only that I trusted my instinct to go, but also that I didn't let my "I can't afford it" excuse stop me from being as resourceful as I was capable of being.

Excuses are dream killers. If we allow them, our excuses will keep us locked in a prison of our own making. As the adage goes, if you argue for your limitations, you get to keep them.

If we really want to, we can all find something to blame for our lack of results. But nothing is more of a deterrent to your long-term success than an untrained mind. Whenever you catch yourself making an excuse, don't buy it. Don't allow any excuse to rent space in your head or heart. Ask yourself, what about the Bethanys or the Tererais or the Malalas of our world? Or the billions of heroic people across the planet who overcome extraordinary challenges each and every day?

They don't have some magical gene you don't. They've simply learned how to tap into their inborn power. The goal is not to compare ourselves to others (always a losing proposition), but to be inspired by our shared humanity.

No matter what you believe your limitations are, I promise that if you look hard enough, you'll find someone with more challenges than you. A lot more. Even Tererai said, "Who am I to complain that I'm feeding my children from trash cans? Where I come from, millions of homeless kids are eating food from trash cans that no one is washing. At least in the American trash can, someone washes it."[5]

Seek out stories of people who can become touchstones for your mental and emotional strength. People whose stories of relentless heart and determination inspire you to dig deeper and keep going. Finding others who have persevered despite difficulties doesn't negate the validity of your hardships. Use those stories to keep your own life in perspective. If they were able to figure it out, so can you.

> You take your life in your own hands, and what happens? A terrible thing: no one to blame.
>
> *Erica Jong*

While I tend to dislike frameworks that ignore the nuances of life, sometimes a clear contrast wakes us up. Here's an adage that serves this conversation well:

There are two kinds of people in the world: those with reasons and those with results.

If you want, you can keep all your reasons (i.e., excuses) why you can't make change happen. Why you can't figure things out. You can hang on to all your reasons—your age, your parents, your genetics, your health, where you were born, ad nauseam. No one is going to come and take those reasons away. You have every right to think and believe whatever you want.

But if you do hold on to the reasons why you "can't," know this: You'll never experience the depth of your love, your gifts, your strength, your creativity, and your highest potential. Neither will the world.

TRUTHS AND TACTICS: OVERCOMING PERCEIVED LIMITATIONS

No problem can withstand the assault of sustained thinking.
Attributed to Voltaire

At this point, you're in one of two camps. Camp 1: You know excuses are weak AF. They're toxic lies that do nothing but strangle your life force. If this describes you, head straight into the Insight to Action Challenge at the end of this chapter.

Or, you're in Camp 2. Philosophically, you're on board, but you need tactical help to shed your day-to-day constraints. Let's dive deep into the three most common excuses: lack of time, money, and know-how. You'll be happy to know that, like everything else, they're all figureoutable.

EXCUSE #1: "I DON'T HAVE THE TIME."

Who doesn't feel time-starved these days? Being "crazy busy," stressed-out, and chronically overwhelmed has become a cultural epidemic. Just because overstuffing our lives with endless to-dos is popular doesn't mean it's wise. Or that it's the only way to live.

Like it or not, we all get the same twenty-four hours in the day. Only you get to decide how you spend it. Yes, I know. We all have jobs. Many of us have multiple jobs, and kids, and spouses, and pets, and parents, and grandparents, and health challenges. Never mind loved ones with special needs, community work, unreliable public transportation, and an ever-growing list of projects and responsibilities. Even with all that, don't get snookered into the "I just don't have the time" mindset.

Whatever your schedule or responsibilities, they didn't just happen. Your life, including how you spend your time, is a by-product of the choices you've made. For better or worse, you played a part in getting yourself here.

To be clear, the difficulties you face right now aren't your fault. There's a difference between owning your choices and blaming yourself. For example, when my stepson was a preteen, sometimes I'd complain about tidying up after him. I was struggling to grow my business and holding down multiple side jobs. Cleaning was *not* how I wanted to spend my free time. I'd throw myself a little pity party and act bitchy, which naturally created tension among Josh, my stepson, and me. That's when I had to remind myself of an important truth: I chose to be with a man who had a young son. That meant, even though I didn't want biological children, some part of me wanted to be a stepmom. How do I know that? Because I am one. I made that choice. And that choice has always been worth the price of admission.

Own your choices. If you take responsibility for how you spend your time, you reclaim the power to change it. Since "not enough time" can be one of the toughest excuse nuts to crack, write this oh-so-important time truth down:

> **If it's important enough, I'll make the time.**
> **If not, I'll make an excuse.**

Say it. Chant it. Sing it. Do whatever it takes to allow this truth to keep you in the driver's seat of your life. The key to demolishing the time excuse is to first embrace the fact that everything you're doing with your twenty-four hours is a choice. Your choice. A choice that you make and a choice you can change. Consider this wild yet true fact:

YOU DO NOT HAVE TO DO ANYTHING IN LIFE.

Everything you do, you choose! And I do mean everything. Feeding yourself. Going to work. Giving the kids a bath. Paying taxes. Staying in a relationship. Responding to emails, or using email at all (some incredibly accomplished humans don't). Participating in social media (again, some very accomplished and happy people don't). Watching the news, TV, or movies. Reading books. Grocery shopping. Answering your phone. Running your business. Doing laundry. Talking with your family. Every single thing you do in life is a choice you're making, whether you realize it or not.

You might say, "This is ridiculous, Marie. I have to pay taxes, otherwise the IRS will find me and cart my ass off to jail!" Or, "I have to give the kids a bath, otherwise they'll turn into little spaghetti-crusted zombies." Or, "I have to go to work, otherwise I'll get fired and lose my house." You're right. There are consequences for not paying your taxes, not bathing your kids, and not showing up for work. But consequences don't negate the fact that you're still making the choice. You're making these choices because they matter to you. And that's the point: You make time for what matters most.

No one is holding a gun to your head and forcing you to read and respond to emails. No one is strong-arming you into watching the news or back-to-back episodes of *The Sopranos*. We choose it. All of it.

As motivational speaker Michael Altshuler says, "The bad news is time flies. The good news is you're the pilot." There is no time fairy that's going to swoop down and magically clear your calendar. Embrace the fact that if you were powerful enough to create an overcommitted and overstretched life, you're powerful enough to uncreate it.

We must focus on the one and only thing we can control in life: ourselves. Our thoughts. Our beliefs. Our feelings. Our behavior.

Remember . . .

**It's never about having the time,
it's about making the time.**

Is changing your ingrained habits easy? No. To free up your time, will you need to say no to people? Disappoint people? Yes. Are you going to disrupt societal norms, ruffle feathers, have uncomfortable conversations, and dismantle a few long-held assumptions? Most definitely.

But here's a good place to start—realize that you can't manage what you don't measure. If you're serious about eradicating time excuses, do this. For the next seven days, write down every single thing you do from the moment you wake up to the moment you go to sleep.

Don't change your normal routine. Record what you typically do, without embellishment or judgment. Your ego may be tempted to fudge the numbers or adjust your behavior to make yourself appear better on paper. Don't do that. The whole point of this exercise is to understand precisely how you spend your time. Plus, you need a baseline of how you're currently spending your time before you can alter it.

Very important: Leave no minute unaccounted for. Be an obsessive, note-taking little freak for the next seven days. Grab a notebook and track your time in two-, ten-, or thirty-minute increments—whatever helps you capture the most accurate snapshot. Include things like lunch breaks, text threads with family, eating hummus over the sink, walking the dog, watering the plants, going to the post office for stamps, grabbing a coffee around the corner, tweezing stray chin hairs.

I guarantee the benefit of seeing exactly where your time goes will far outweigh the effort. Most of us don't realize how much time we fritter away on dumb shit that has no connection to our deepest values nor moves the needle ahead on our treasured dreams. What's worse, modern environments are designed to distract us, fracture our time, and steal our attention.

The result we're ultimately aiming for? Freeing up two hours a day. Before you throw this book against the wall or think, *You're out of your damn mind, Marie! I can't find an extra two minutes, let alone two hours a day,* stick with me and, at the very least, experiment. As you track your time, pay particular attention to our society's biggest time sucks:

- Social media (no surprise there)
- Email
- The internet in general (shopping, scrolling through news, going down the rabbit hole)
- Inefficient meal planning and prep

- Traffic and commuting
- Meetings (many of which don't really add value to our jobs, or could be more quickly and effectively addressed in email)
- Television (yes, Netflix counts)
- Running errands (that are not essential or could be done later when they're less distracting to our most creative, high-energy hours)
- Being on your cell phone for whatever reason (e.g., talking, texting, gaming, watching YouTube videos, or listening to podcasts)

This last bullet deserves extra attention. Few of us can imagine a world without smartphones. We wake up with them. We take them to the bathroom. We go to bed with them. We have them at the dinner table. Billions of us are addicted to screens. If you haven't noticed, technology now controls us more than we control it. While everyone is unique in their tech usage, one recent study estimates Americans now spend nearly five hours a day on their phones. That's seventy-six days a year—roughly a third of our waking lives—glued to a glowing box!

This addiction to technology isn't by accident, it's by design. Devices are built to keep you hooked. Every color, sound, and feature is intentionally engineered to get you to spend more and more time on your screen.

Companies with billions of dollars employ some of the most intelligent, creative humans on the planet to mastermind new ways to lure us into spending our lives on their apps and in their platforms. Remember, stock prices rely on keeping engagement metrics high. Many tech companies' survival is based on continuously inventing ways to capture an ever-growing share of your time and attention. If you think you're a customer of these products and platforms, think again. Your time, attention, and data are their product.

Here's how it works. Your brain interprets every text, alert, or like as a "reward," which triggers a dopamine surge. Over time, those chemicals change how your mind functions, *training you* to need more and more "dopamine hits" from your devices. It's a feedback loop that's almost impossible to resist.

The most addictive platforms get us hooked by exploiting five universal psychological vulnerabilities: the slot machine effect of getting intermittent, variable rewards ("Did I get a new email, text, or DM!?"); the need to be seen ("Notice me, acknowledge me, like me, love me!!"); the need to reciprocate ("I have to respond and say thanks—can't seem rude!"); the fear of missing out (FOMO); and our most masochistic impulse—to constantly compare ourselves to others (what I call doing shots of Comparschläger*).

It doesn't matter how many hours a day you meditate or how intellectually or spiritually superior you think you are, everyone is susceptible. Steve Jobs knew this all too well. That's why he wouldn't let his kids use iPads. When the tablet first hit the shelves in 2010, *New York Times* journalist Nick Bilton asked this of Mr. Jobs, "So, your kids must love the iPad?"

"They haven't used it," he told Nick. "We limit how much technology our kids use at home." Nick's article went on to detail how a fair number of technocrats follow similar screen-limiting practices. Chris Anderson, the CEO of 3DR and former editor of *Wired* magazine, put stringent device rules in place for his family. "My kids accuse me and my wife of being fascists and overly concerned about tech, and they say that none of their friends have the same rules," he said of his five chil-

---

*Comparschläger: noun; a self-inflicted poison. Activates when you compare yourself to others and end up feeling worthless. Analogous to Goldschläger, the disgusting cinnamon-flavored schnapps with gold flakes that, when ingested in large quantities, makes you puke.

dren, aged six to seventeen. "That's because we have seen the dangers of technology firsthand. I've seen it in myself, I don't want to see that happen to my kids."[6]

It begs the question: If some of the world's most powerful tech pioneers don't allow unlimited screen time in their homes, why should we? I'm not demonizing our devices—I'm grateful for the countless benefits technology has brought to my life and to humanity—but appreciating the upside doesn't negate the hazards.

Most of us are grossly unaware of how much time we actually spend on our screens. Research shows that we're likely to underestimate our phone usage by nearly 50 percent. According to psychologist Sally Andrews, a lecturer at Nottingham Trent University and the lead author of a smartphone study, "The fact that we use our phones twice as many times as we think we do indicates that a lot of smartphone use seems to be habitual, automatic behaviors that we have no awareness of."[7]

When I started to become suspect of my own habits, I genuinely believed I was on my phone far less than I was. My wake-up call? A free app called Moment.* It tracks your phone and app usage and shows you exactly how much time you stare at your little addiction box each day. Prepare to be horrified.

Let's say you're a holdout and scoff at so-called smartphones. I respect that. But don't think you're off the hook. Nielsen shows that, on average, American adults are still watching some five hours of TV a day. A DAY.

Even if you've sworn off all screens and tech and you're living like it's 1926, do the time-tracking exercise for the full seven days. Get curious about exactly what you do and how long it takes. Research has proven

---

*Apple now has a native feature called Screen Time that functions much the same way.

that roughly 40 percent of our daily activities are habitual. Which means we humans spend a significant portion of our existence on auto-pilot with no awareness of what the hell we're doing when we're doing it.

Remember, your mission is to free up at least two hours a day. Why two, you ask? First, because two hours a day is enough of a stretch that it forces you to challenge deeply held assumptions about how you've constructed your life. My hope is to inspire you to have some uncomfortable-yet-necessary conversations with yourself, family, friends, and coworkers. Whether it's about finding ways to be more effective in less time, rebalancing responsibilities, or setting boundaries, use this as an opportunity to communicate what you need and enlist support.

Second, because the cumulative effect of spending two hours every day toward a meaningful goal will alter the trajectory of your life. Honestly, even if you don't free up two hours but end up with one, that's enormous progress. Over the course of a year, you'll have created an additional two weeks of free time.*

Push yourself. If you don't strive for two free hours a day, chances are you won't even get one.

---

*365/24 hours = 15.20 full 24-hour days. If we make this waking focused time, you'd have an extra 45 8-hour workdays per year.

You Can Get with This, or You Can Get with *That*

THE OPPORTUNITY COST OF WASTING YOUR TIME

Today's Unconscious Cost	Total Time Spent per Year	What You Could've Accomplished Instead
30 minutes a day dickin' around on your phone/social media	182.5 hours a year or *22 full 8-hour workdays*	Michelle-Obama-like arms Built a brand-new website Learned how to meditate
60 minutes a day on news, email, and celebrity gossip	365 hours a year or *45 full 8-hour workdays*	Written a first draft of your book Launched a new revenue stream Secured a raise or made a career change
90 minutes a day watching TV	547.5 hours a year or *68 full 8-hour workdays*	Learned to speak conversational Italian Finished your degree Launched a profitable side business

Opportunity cost is no joke. Every choice has a price. Everything you say yes to means you're saying no to something else. Translation? Each time you pick up your brain-draining gadget and say *YES* to watching another cat video, you're saying *NOPE* to ever reaching your biggest and most important long-term goals.

Want to speak another language? Write a book? Transform your body or health? Get your financial life together? Launch any kind of business, side hustle, or a whole new career? Save the oceans? Find time for a real relationship? Reignite your sex life? You absolutely have the time, right now.

The thirty minutes a day you spend screen sucking your phone could be used to get in a HIIT workout and take your fitness level from "blah" to "badass" in a matter of months.

The hour you spend browsing the internet for more shit you don't need could be used to write a few paragraphs of your memoir. You'd have a workable first draft within a year.

The two hours you spend watching mind-numbing TV each night could instead be used to learn a new language, study for that degree, or work on a relationship you really care about.

I can hear some of you saying, "Okay, Marie, I see your point. But I still can't see how to find two hours a day." Remember, thirty minutes here and fifteen minutes there add up fast.

Here are a few more strategies to kill the time sucks mentioned above. You don't have to make these changes permanently. Some might not be possible given your job or life situation, but I strongly encourage you to experiment with a few—if not all—for one month. You can do anything for thirty days. Use these suggestions as jumping-off points to invent your own experiments. Remember to ask, "How can this work for me?"

Nothing changes if nothing changes. Be bold. Break your patterns.

Step away from societal norms that suffocate your life. With a few tweaks, you'll see how possible more free time really is.

1. Eliminate Media Consumption

Eliminate all media including social media, TV, online videos, magazines, catalogs, podcasts, news, and any other information-based inputs. If the thought of no media is making you hyperventilate, relax. Go on a media fast for four weeks. You'll survive. After that, you can create better boundaries for your consumption (e.g., no media before 11:00 a.m. so you can capitalize on morning energy).

Here's the mantra I use to curb my own media consumption: **"Create before you consume."** Meaning, it's imperative that I create the life (and work) of my dreams before I unconsciously and habitually consume the creations of others. For example, ten minutes of meditation helps me create a stronger brain and experience more clarity, insights, and creativity; a fifteen-minute home workout can help me create more energy and strength; twenty-five minutes of writing can help me chip away at a book or marketing idea and create major progress in my career. Heck, even five minutes of quiet thinking—distraction-free—creates breakthroughs!

Which highlights an important point. Yes, I'm challenging you to carve out two free hours a day. As your coach on this journey, I'm here to push you. But even upgrading your behavior in small pockets of time—five minutes here, fifteen minutes there—will give you small wins to build on, the cumulative effect of which creates miracles. Ten minutes is better than no minutes.

2. Break Out of Your Inbox

Put up a vacationesque autoresponder and limit email checking to one to three times per day, maximum. Do not check email right after you wake up. If you can check every few days, even better. This is admittedly easier for entrepreneurs and freelancers than it is for some employees, but difficult does not mean impossible. As a boss, I encourage my team members to declare times when they'll be in focus mode (not available via email or Slack) for multi-hour chunks—sometimes full days—in order to make progress on important projects, distraction-free.

Even if it's not possible at work, how can this idea help curb your personal inbox? Whatever changes you make, inform family, close friends, coworkers, and top clients about your new email policy. Chances are, they'll respect it. Once key people are in the know and you turn on your autoresponder, do NOT open your inbox.

The best way to break a compulsive email-checking habit is to set up your environment to support you. That means removing visual and audio email temptations completely. If possible, delete the email app from your phone. If you're unwilling, take your email app off the home screen of your smartphone and move it to at least the fourth or fifth screen. The few seconds it takes to swipe over to *find* that email icon can be enough of a pattern interrupt to stop you from habitually checking it.

The most important thing is eliminating all notifications from any device or computer you use. No dings, buzzes, swooshes, notifications, or visual pop-ups. This is nonnegotiable. Take back control over your mind, time, and attention. Do not allow your technology to dictate your to-do list. Other people's agendas shouldn't derail your own.

The world has been writing extensively about how to better manage email since the year 2000. Search online and you'll find a treasure trove of email-taming tools and practices.

3. Eat Better, Faster, and Cheaper

For some of us, one of the biggest recurring time sucks is feeding our-selves and our families. Figuring out what to eat, and then shopping, prepping, cooking, and cleaning up—it feels like a whole other job.

I'm sure you know this, but a nonstop diet of fast, processed, pack-aged foods is not a viable, long-term option. I say this as someone who grew up on Chef Boyardee, Pasta Roni, peanut butter cups, Pop-Tarts, pizza, and White Castle. It wasn't until my late twenties that I realized the error of my ways. Processed food drains your energy, clouds your cognitive abilities, and triggers a host of mental, physical, and emotional health issues.

If figuring out what to eat is one of your biggest time sucks, try this. Learn to batch cook and embrace being boring and repetitive with your meals. Find three to five simple, whole-food-based recipes that can be made in large quantities (soups, stews, one-pot meals, bowls) and desig-nate two times a week (e.g., Thursdays and Sundays) to plan, shop, prep, and execute. There's an ever-growing free library of healthy, fast, and easy-to-prepare recipes and how-tos online.

Let's talk money, too. Here's another myth we need to debunk. You don't have to shop in expensive health-food stores or farmers' markets, or eat only organic foods. The goal is to select the healthiest options possible, no matter where you shop. *New York Times* columnist Mark Bittman wrote an insightful 2010 op-ed called "Is Junk Food Really Cheaper?" In it, he explained that to feed a family of four at McDonald's costs about twenty-eight dollars. To feed a family of four a roast chicken with vegetables and a simple salad costs about fourteen dollars. To feed a family of four rice and beans with garlic, peppers, and onions costs about nine dollars. Search for "The Environmental Working Group's Guide for Good Food on a Tight Budget" or follow their Clean Fifteen and Dirty Dozen lists for fruits and vegetables. These resources help us eat well and save money. Remember, everything is figureoutable— including fueling yourself and family with real, nutrient-dense food without breaking the bank.

The goal here is to reframe the way you think about and approach eating. Strive to simplify and remove daily decision making (*I don't know, what do* you *want to eat tonight?!*) as much as possible. With a mental shift and a bit of planning, you can have a house that's stocked with healthy leftovers and nutrient-rich, no-prep-time-needed snacks like nuts, fruits, and vegetables.

Wouldn't you agree that experimenting with just a few of these ideas, even for just a few weeks, could open up a fresh perspective on how you spend your time?

If you need one last push to carve out two free hours a day, here you go . . .

If you had to find the time, you would.

Imagine your doctor called to say that you have a rare, life-threatening disease. The only chance for a full recovery: You must sit quietly and uninterrupted for two hours a day, seven days a week for the next three months. No smartphones, no social media, no television or computer time. Just two free hours a day without interruption, or your life will come to an abrupt end.

How would you do it? What changes would you make to create two free, uninterrupted hours each day for the next ninety days? Would checking social feeds or email really seem that important? Be honest. If your life *depended* on it, you'd absolutely find two free hours per day.

Now that we've annihilated our time excuses, let's tackle money.

EXCUSE #2: "I DON'T HAVE THE MONEY."

One of my favorite Tony Robbins quotes is: "It's never about your resources, it's about your resourcefulness." This philosophy is applicable to all excuses, but especially financial.

Let's start off with a question: What exactly do you believe you need more money for? Is it at all possible you might be able to get to your end result without paying full price, or any price at all? For example, let's say you think you need money to learn a new skill or start a new career. That's not necessarily true. With access to the internet, you can develop virtually any new skill set, often for free.

Robotics, programming, math, negotiation, statistics, design, knitting—all online. The amount of high-quality, free education available through apps, videos, podcasts, blogs, and MOOCs (massive online open courses) is staggering and constantly growing. The website edX is a learning destination with free online courses from the best universities and institutions like Harvard, MIT, UC Berkeley, and more. Khan Academy, whose mission is to provide free world-class education for anyone, anywhere, tackles subjects like math, science, computer programming, history, art history, and economics. The New York University School of Medicine recently announced that it would cover the tuition, regardless of merit or need, for all current and future students.[8]

Maybe you want to start your own business. Do you think you need piles of cash to get your company off the ground? Decades ago, perhaps. But we're living in a different time. In fact, I've been asked a version of

"Marie, how can I start my own business if I don't have money?" so many times that I created a list of over 320 free tools and platforms that can help virtually any small-business owner get going immediately. It's a resource that's been downloaded and shared hundreds of thousands of times. Search *Marie Forleo + free tools resources.*

Now let's say you want to launch a business that *does* require capital. If you're determined, creative, and relentless enough, there are a host of ways to get the financing you need. You'll need to explore every legal and ethical option, but if you're committed, you'll make it happen. Here are a handful of ideas to spark your imagination.

Side Jobs. When it comes to needing more money, this has always been my method of choice. When I was growing up, my dad would often say, "I've never once opened the newspaper and not seen a Help Wanted section." That taught me to see the world as a place where driven, hardworking, responsible people are always in demand. He taught me that doing honest work, no matter the task, was something to be proud of. As long as I showed up with a can-do attitude and went above and beyond, I'd always be able to find work.

When I first started my business, I was tens of thousands of dollars in debt. In order to get the money I needed for my first website, I worked extra shifts at the bar and saved for it. In fact, I worked multiple side jobs for seven full years before I was financially stable enough to run my business full-time.

Yes, you have to be industrious. Yes, you have to be bold. Yes, you have to be humble. (I never expected to be cleaning toilets after college, but I did it and was grateful for the work.) Plus, what better way to build the reputation of someone willing to do whatever it takes? What better way to build a network? Have you ever noticed that those are exactly the kind of people who succeed in life?

Spend Less. My friend is the CEO of a financial education company and a single mom of two kids. She moved her family from a big, expensive house into a small, modest apartment. That move enabled her to slash her monthly expenses to a fraction of what they'd been, instantly freeing up significant cash flow to save and invest for her family's future. While they initially worried that downsizing would mean suffering, the exact opposite happened. Emotionally, her family grew closer than ever. They became more engaged in each other's lives and felt happier and calmer with less stuff weighing them down.

You might consider a more radical move. A couple who enrolled in B-School, my online business program, decided they wanted to test several different business ideas and have the freedom to fail, pivot, or change their minds without fear of running out of money. After crunching the numbers, they realized that testing various ideas would be near impossible while living in an expensive area like Brooklyn, New York. So they mapped a plan, put their furniture in storage, and moved to a startup-friendly country in South America where their living expenses were a fraction of what they would have been in New York. While that decision may seem extreme, that kind of thinking is required if you want to break free from your money excuses and figure out your dreams.

Sell Stuff. Go old school and have a garage sale. Or use sites like eBay or Craigslist to sell what you have to generate additional cash. I once had a woman so determined to come to a live training event that she sold her couch to pay for her ticket.

Scholarships and Grants. According to a study on Pell Grants, around $2.9 billion in US federal grants—which don't have to be paid back—went unused in 2014 alone.[9] There are tremendous resources available in the form of scholarships and grants, as long as you use the figure-outable philosophy and do the work.

One of my favorite examples is from a woman named Gabrielle McCormick. Her basketball scholarship disappeared after she ruptured her Achilles tendon her senior year. Disappointed but still determined, she channeled her pain into finding new financial possibilities.

She discovered that you can earn scholarships for almost anything, from playing video games to drawing birds to wearing contact lenses to making your prom dress out of duct tape. Her efforts earned her over $150,000 in scholarships. She graduated with zero debt and secured scholarships to pay for her doctorate degree. In addition to her studies, Gabrielle also runs a business called Scholarship Informer to help parents and students avoid loans and debt. Worth taking the time to figure out, right?

Crowdfunding. Sites like Kickstarter, Indiegogo, and GoFundMe are some of the more well-known sites connecting people who want to financially support projects, companies, and individuals. Do a quick search for *top crowdfunding sites + [current year]* and you'll see an ever-growing array of platforms, from peer-to-peer lending to education funding sites to equity investing and more.

The List Goes On. What stops you is never external. Ever. It's never about the lack of money or time or anything else. It's about your internal game, your commitment to do whatever it takes to be creative, get resourceful, and figure it out. To find or make a way ahead, no matter what.

EXCUSE #3: "I DON'T KNOW HOW/I DON'T KNOW WHERE TO START."

We're not going to spend much time on this excuse because, honestly, it's weak.

We live in the most unprecedented time in human history. With the ever-growing miracle known as the internet, you can learn the fundamentals of virtually any topic or skill within minutes, often 100 percent free of charge and in the privacy of your own home. In their book *Abundance,* authors Peter Diamandis and Steven Kotler write, "Right now a Masai warrior with a cell phone has better mobile phone capabilities than the president of the United States did twenty-five years ago. And if he's on a smart phone with access to Google, then he has better access to information than the president did just fifteen years ago."

No matter what it is that you want to learn, your answer likely already exists. It's already been explained in a book, online, or in some form of media. Or it can be learned directly from another person through a class, tutoring, mentorship, apprenticeship, etc. Or you might arrive at an aha moment through meditation, prayer, journaling, or even a spontaneous insight in the shower.

In this day and age, there's no shortage of information available to you. Once you commit and get started, use every idea in this chapter and the rest of the book to keep going until you figure it out!

The art of eliminating excuses means embracing the fact that your dreams aren't made or broken by anyone but you.

INSIGHT TO ACTION CHALLENGE

Put your ass where your heart wants to be.
Steven Pressfield

1. *What's an instance where, at first, you believed you didn't have the time, ability, or resources to make something happen, and yet you figured it out anyway?* List as many as you can remember. No example is too small or insignificant.

2. *What's the most important goal you're ready to solve, achieve, or figure out?* (Hint: What did you come up with in the last chapter? Write it down again. Repetition has power.)

3. *What are the top three excuses that—before this chapter—you would have used to stop yourself?*

4. *Now cross out each excuse.* ~~SLASH IT THROUGH.~~ One by one write down why each excuse is no longer valid. Then write what you're now willing to think, say, or do instead to eliminate that excuse.

   Excuse #1: ~~I don't have the time to get my PhD.~~

Why Excuse #1 is a lie: If my PhD was really that important, I'd make the time. I'd quit binge-watching Netflix, go to sleep before 11:00 p.m., and wake up earlier each day. I'd quit mindless social media. I'd batch cook. I'd have a conversation with my partner about how important this goal is to me and brainstorm how we can make it happen as a team.

What I can think/say/do instead: I always make time for what matters.

Action: Make radical changes in my schedule. Start researching PhD programs today. If I'm not willing to do this, then it's time to stop talking about it and find a new goal that lights up my heart.

5. ***Seven-day time tracking.*** If not enough time is your main-squeeze excuse, track your time for the next seven days. Review the previous recommendations. If you use a smartphone or tablet, download the free app Moment (or enable Screen Time on iOS) and track your screen time and app usage.

MONDAY

Time	Activity	Notes/Insights
6:30–6:57 a.m.	Wake up and check phone	I check news, Twitter, and Instagram. Why exactly?
6:57–7:06 a.m.	Turn on the coffee, fire up the laptop, close extra tabs in browser	I habitually check email again on my laptop without even thinking

Time	Activity	Notes/Insights
7:07–7:14 a.m.	Shower	
7:15–7:19 a.m.	Check phone	Respond to texts, check social
7:19–7:46 a.m.	Get dressed, fix hair, etc.	

At the end of seven days, review your time log, and (if applicable) the stats on your Moment app or Screen Time on iOS. Use the following questions to take an objective look at how you're spending your most precious resource. Not all prompts will be relevant. Use them as thought starters to create your own.

- On a scale of 1 to 10, how much does this activity serve my most important values and goals? (1 = it works *against* what you say you most want. 10 = it fully aligns with your values and goals.)
- Does this activity really need to be done? If yes, how could it be done faster or less frequently? Could it be batched or automated? Could it be done by someone else?
- What's the best thing that could happen if I stopped doing this—either temporarily or permanently? What are the best possible short-term and long-term consequences?
- What's the worst thing that could happen if I stopped doing this—either temporarily or permanently? What are the worst probable short-term and long-term consequences?

6. *If you had to, you would: Write down your life-saving, two-free-hours-a-day plan.* Remember, your doctor called. She said the only chance you have to save your own life is sitting quietly and uninterrupted for two hours a day, seven days a week for the next three months. There is no other cure. How would you do it?

Bonus Wordplay Challenge

The words you think, say, and reinforce will become your reality. Anytime you catch yourself making excuses or saying, "I can't," STOP. Challenge that thought. Is it really true that you can't? Or is it more true that you *won't?* Or that you don't want to? This isn't semantics. When you say, "I can't," you're sending yourself an internal message that you're not in control of your time or choices. Replace "I can't" with something more honest, like "I don't want to."

For bonus points, do this now. Think of something you've wanted to achieve or experience in the past but have made excuses about. Then, say the following phrases out loud:

> The truth is . . .
> I don't really want it that bad.
> It's not a priority right now.
> It's not that important.
> I'm not willing to work that hard/take the risk/put in the effort/etc.
> That's okay.

(Seriously. Say these out loud!)
See how much better that feels?

Bonus Must-Watch *MarieTV*s

1. *No Excuses Episode.* I have a character named Jersey Marie who made a very special video about the power of living an excuse-free life. Search *Marie Forleo No Excuses* whenever you need a one-of-a-kind excuse smackdown.

2. *How to Achieve an Impossible Dream with Dr. Tererai Trent.* It's hard to describe how impactful it is to hear Dr. Trent tell her story. Search *Marie Forleo + Tererai Trent* for one of the most moving, inspiring, and uplifting interviews ever. Grab your tissue box.

Above all, be the heroine of
your life, not the victim.

Nora Ephron

Figureoutable Field Notes

This twenty-three-year-old single mom with no education past tenth grade used everything is figureoutable *to get her GED and a bachelor's degree and is now in law school—all while holding down a full-time job as a communications director at a major global bank.*

When I came across Marie, I was a twenty-three-year-old mother with no education past tenth grade. I had my daughter in high school, but before that I was an athlete and a brilliant writer, with the core wiring of an entrepreneur.

Becoming a parent forced me to put my dreams on hold and provide my daughter with everything she needed to begin her own life. When her dad and I split, I had a choice: I could be upset and full of sorrow, or I could answer my nagging entrepreneur, locked away and barred from creativity due to the responsibility of parenting.

The nagging was so annoying, and YouTube being the distraction it is, I thought I'd search for something impossible: "Chasing unrealistic dreams." Marie's video "Dream Big: 5 Steps to Help You Chase Your Most 'Unrealistic' Dreams" was the top hit. I clicked on the video. My breakthrough was seconds away.

The concept *everything is figureoutable* gave me hope when there

(continued)

was none. Marie helped me realize that if I do the work, I can have whatever I desire in this life. My family has decades of limiting beliefs, and I was aching to break them. I knew I was bright, and I wanted to finish what I started. Even though I was a parent, my soul wouldn't allow that limitation to define me.

Since watching that first video, I got my GED and a bachelor's degree in legal studies, and now I'm a single mother in LAW SCHOOL maintaining a full-time job as a communications director at a major global bank.

I participate in a global leadership development program and have become the regional leader in my company's diversity and inclusion network for African American employees nationwide.

Everything is figureoutable. There are so many steps that led me here, but HOPE inspired by Marie's video reminded me that nothing was impossible when I needed to hear it the most. I can't imagine where I'd be if I hadn't come across Marie that day, but I am deeply grateful that I did. I share this concept with my team every day!

—AVELYN
MASSACHUSETTS

5

How to Deal with the Fear of Anything

Nothing in life is to be feared, it is only to be understood. Now is the time to understand more, so that we may fear less.

Attributed to Marie Curie

Josh and I were on Salina, a beautiful island off the coast of Sicily where the best way to get around is by scooter. I hadn't ridden a scooter for at least twenty years, but I was excited to get back on one. It was a blazing hot day in July, so I was wearing shorts as we walked from our hotel over to the scooter rental joint. Despite my heritage, my Italian is not stellar, and the owner of the rental shop didn't speak much English. Using Google Translate and our best pantomime, I understood her primary question: "Are you familiar with riding scooters?" My response: "No. Please show me *everything*."

She proceeded to give me a brief tutorial. Essentially, she showed me the simple throttle-turning motion, "like-a *dis* to give ah-gas-ah" and a squeeze of the handles "like-a *dis* to brake-ah." Sounds easy enough. *Facile.*

I strapped on my helmet, turned the ignition, and got ready to ride off into paradise. What I didn't realize was that the right lever was the brake for the front wheel and the left lever was the brake for the back wheel. I'm still not quite sure how I managed to do this (such a genius), but I gassed it (hard), panicked, and squeezed *both* brakes at the same time.

In under three seconds I zoomed, crashed, flipped, and landed on the asphalt with bare knees and a 250-pound scooter on top of me. Thank God there were no cars coming. Josh and the folks from the rental place heaved the scooter upright and pulled me to the side of the road. Miraculously, I didn't break any bones. I wasn't bleeding. I was just shaken up and engulfed by a tidal wave of shame and embarrassment. *What a total idiot.*

Understandably, the owner didn't want me back on the road. She offered Josh a bigger scooter so I could relax and ride on the back of his. At that moment, I had a choice to (A) take it easy and be the passenger or (B) get my ass up, climb back on, and learn to ride without killing myself or anyone else.

I chose B. Here's why.

You never get stronger if you only do easy things. I didn't want fear to calcify in my bones. I refuse to energetically shrink down into a smaller, less capable me. Just because I made a mistake and *messed* up didn't mean I was going to *give* up.

So I took a deep breath and got back on the scooter (yes, I was still shaking). But this time, in painstaking detail, I had everyone explain to me exactly what to do and what *not* to do. Very slowly, I tried again. Then I did little test runs up and down a side road. By the end of the day, I was able to zip around the island with relative ease. Within a few days, I was having the time of my life.

Here's something you can never hear enough: we all wipe out. Physically, emotionally, creatively, financially, socially—everyone does dumb shit. It's inherent to the human growth process. But here's the key: a fall is never final unless you stay on the ground.

You might have heard that "fear" is the acronym for False Evidence Appearing Real. Or maybe you roll with the cheeky edition: Fuck Everything and Run. I prefer the more actionable version: Face Everything and Rise. Let's take a closer look at fear and the multitude of ways we can metabolize, manage, and mitigate it as we continue on our figureoutable journey.

THE F-WORD YOU NEED
TO EMBRACE

Thank God for fear. If it didn't exist, we'd all be dead.

In this chapter, we're not talking about the fear that keeps us alive (e.g., fear of standing in front of a speeding train). We're talking about fear that keeps us small and stuck. Fear is one of the most misunderstood F-words. Left unexamined, it's a dream killer. A soul squelcher. The grand maester of mediocrity. If this were *Family Feud* and Steve Harvey asked, "What stops us humans from achieving our highest potential?" survey says fear would take the top spot.

Guess what? Everyone feels afraid. Every top artist, athlete, writer, performer, parent, businessperson, social activist, entrepreneur, scientist, and military leader. Newbies to icons. Every person you know and admire. They all experience fear on a regular basis. You're not broken or weak if you're afraid. You're human.

But this begs the question: Why does fear paralyze some people while others move through it? This one ability is what separates those who aspire from those who achieve. In this chapter, you're going to become part of the latter group. Fear, like everything else, is figure-outable.

And figure it out you must, because no matter what you want to explore, change, or overcome, fear will surface throughout your journey. The good news is that unexamined fear is like unmined gold. It contains riches for those wise and patient enough to pan through the dirt.

Obviously, it's impossible for me to know what specific fear is holding you back.* Even if I did, there's no one-size-fits-all approach that works for every person in every situation. Fear comes in many flavors and intensities, from sweaty palms and knotty tummies to nightmare scenarios in your head to full-blown phobias. Add to that, we all have our own pet names for fear—concern, stress, anxiety, panic, terror, and stage fright, just to name a few. Finally, we each bring our own unique and layered emotional history into the mix, from childhood trauma and teenage humiliation to a tapestry of emotional experiences accumulated throughout our adult lives. All this is to state the obvious: fear is complex and multifaceted. Which is why it's the sole focus of many outstanding books, courses, and therapies.

Transforming your fear is more art than science. Different approaches work for different people. Which is why you should mix, match, and experiment with the following suggestions. They're a blend of cognitive, emotional, and somatic strategies that can transform any fear into productive, creative fuel. I've used and taught them over the years, so I know all of them work when used in good faith. Let's begin with an important paradigm shift.

---

*The two most common are (1) the fear of not being good enough and (2) the fear you won't be loved. Got either? Welcome to the club.

FEAR IS NOT THE ENEMY

> There are very few monsters who warrant the fear we
> have of them.
>
> *André Gide*

Our first and biggest mistake is that we've turned fear into the enemy. A big, burly, malignant monster standing between us and our dreams. But what if this idea is not only wrong, but doing us more harm than good? What if we've been taught to believe a disempowering story about this natural emotion that's actually designed to serve us, not stop us?

Fear is an evolutionary response that kept our ancestors from being eaten by tigers. These days, that same instinct prevents us from walking into ongoing traffic. Helpful, to say the least. But fear is always helpful if properly understood.

Your fear doesn't need to be "crushed" or annihilated. It needs to be listened to and appreciated for the gift it offers. Think about an infant who wails in her crib or a dog who incessantly barks. They're trying their best to communicate *something*, they just don't have the language skills to articulate it.

The same is true with fear. Fear communicates using the only tool she has: the ability to make you feel. When you sense her presence, she's sounding a compassionate alarm. She's doing her best to get you to pay attention. This subtle yet important distinction will help you put down your combat gear and, instead, meet your fear with open arms and a smile.

Fear is not the enemy. Waiting to stop feeling afraid is.

One more time, because it's critical. Fear is not the enemy—waiting to stop feeling afraid is. Spending too much time trying to "defeat" or "eliminate" your fear will only keep you stuck. Fear will be your companion as long as you're alive. It doesn't matter how much experience, success, or fame you acquire. You will always feel fear. Don't get seduced into thinking some magical day will arrive when you no longer feel afraid and only then will you be ready to act. That's not how it works. **Action is the antidote to fear.** Action metabolizes it. The trick is allowing yourself to feel fear while you take action.

Make the call, even if your pits are sweating. Speak up, even if your voice shakes. Ride the scooter, even if your body trembles. Raise your rates, even if it makes you want to hurl. Send your pitch deck, even if your tummy is in knots. Have the difficult conversation, even if it makes you squirm. Doing the thing is far easier than the terror we inflict upon ourselves by stressing over it in our heads. The fastest way out of our fear is through it.

Fear is healthy if it inspires you to act. If the fear of losing custody of your kids gets you clean and sober, say thank you. Fear guided you back to love. If the fear of being suffocated under a pile of debt inspires you to get your financial act together, say thank you. Fear gave birth to freedom. If the fear of having a fatal heart attack before your grandkids graduate helps you eat more veggies, say thank you. Fear just gave you a longer, healthier life.

Fear is your ally. She's a caring messenger and supportive friend—and she's always got your back.

FEAR IS YOUR SOUL'S GPS

> Most misunderstandings in the world could be avoided if people would simply take the time to ask, "What else could this mean?"
>
> *Shannon L. Alder*

Nine times out of ten, our fear is directive. It's a signpost, pointing us in the exact direction our soul wants to go.

How do you know if your fear is directive (as opposed to keeping you alive)? One sign is if you can't get a certain idea out of your heart or mind. No matter how hard you try, it keeps popping back. Ideas like taking singing lessons, opening a bakery, writing a children's book, moving across the country, learning Spanish, running for local office, saving or ending a relationship—you know, any number of delightful or risky creative endeavors.

Anytime you imagine moving toward that idea, you may feel afraid. But fear doesn't speak with words, she's doing her best to send a message by making you *feel*. And this is where we often get it wrong. We interpret any fear-like sensation to mean, "Danger. Stop. Don't move ahead." On cue, the voice in our head rattles off a list of rationalizations designed to keep us away from the perceived danger:

Are you NUTS? Just don't.
You're way too old for that.
You're too young—who's going to take you seriously?

Can't you just be grateful for what you have?

Your time has passed. Accept it.

You have NO clue how to start.

You're not focused enough.

You've got zero follow-through.

You'll wind up in massive debt.

You'll get torn apart online.

You can't afford this.

You'll ruin everything you've worked so hard for.

Stay in your lane.

You don't have the talent.

Everyone's done it already. Way better.

What a stupid idea.

The result? We take no action. Zero growth occurs. Comfort zone intact.

But what if we misinterpreted the signal? What if fear's message wasn't "Danger" but "DO IT!" Fear was jumping up and down, waving her hands and causing the biggest ruckus she could: *YES! YES! YES! This is important!! Go ahead—do THIS thing!* Fear did her job and sent her signal. It was our interpretation that was off.

In his game-changing book *The War of Art,* Steven Pressfield writes:

> The more scared we are of a work or calling, the more sure we
> can be that we have to do it . . . Therefore the more fear we feel
> about a specific enterprise, the more certain we can be that that
> enterprise is important to us and to the growth of our soul.

From this perspective, our fear is supportive and directive, not shameful or weak. Certainly not something to ignore. In fact, we should appreciate the fact that we're getting such clear, visceral guidance. We've tapped a vein of gold. Think about it. If an idea in your heart invokes that much visceral reaction, doesn't it mean there must be *something* worth exploring?

Just because your soul wants to pursue something doesn't mean it's going to be easy. I guarantee it won't be. Check the control panel, put on your crash helmet, and strap yourself in. You're going on an adventure. Expect joy, tears, surprises, confusion, stumbles, and plenty of breakthroughs (and breakdowns) along the way. The figureoutable philosophy doesn't promise a life free from pain, just one free from regret.

When you know in your bones that, no matter what comes your way, you'll be able to figure it out, taking risks becomes a lot less scary. In fact, saying "Everything is figureoutable" out loud is an effective tool for talking yourself off the ledge of self-doubt. Repeat it like a sacred mantra. (I do.) It calms your nervous system and focuses your mind.

Everything is figureoutable.
Everything is figureoutable.
Everything is figureoutable.

You might say: "But what about the very real fear of not being able to pay my rent or making a stupid, irreversible mistake that ruins the rest of my life—and maybe the lives of people I love?"

Great question. Here's how we take direct aim at those.

FEAR TAMING 101

> If a fear cannot be articulated, it can't be conquered.
> *Stephen King*

One reason our fears become so debilitating is that they're vague. We don't slow down enough to thoroughly question them or assess their probability—so we have no idea how likely they are to come true. Nor do we have a practical plan to respond if they do. It's the equivalent of closing our eyes, sticking our fingers in our ears, and screaming, "LA LA LA LA LA LA LA!"—in hope that our fears will magically disappear on their own. Avoidance doesn't extinguish your fear, action does.

Here's what to do instead. Write down the worst, worst, *worst*-case scenario that could possibly happen if you move ahead with this exciting-yet-fear-inducing idea. Dig into it. Next, rate it on a scale of one to ten in terms of the likelihood that this worst-case scenario will occur, with one being improbable and ten being it's practically guaranteed to happen. Finally, imagine the worst-case scenario—your worst nightmare—does indeed come true. Then what? Write down an action plan for how you'd recover, rebuild, and get back on your feet.

I did a simplified version of this when I started my business. My worst-case scenario was total failure and humiliation. In practical terms, I wouldn't make enough money to sustain myself. I'd waste years of my life on a failed venture. I'd be the laughingstock of my friends and would disappoint my family. I'd spend the rest of my life bartending and doing odd jobs.

I challenged myself to go even further. What if that worst-case scenario happened and things got so bad that I lost my bartending job, too? What then? I realized that my ultimate fear was losing everything and not being able to support myself. I imagined what it would be like having no money, no job, and no place to live. That was the worst of the worst for me, *being ashamed, alone, broke, and homeless.*

Now if that worst-worst-worst-case scenario actually happened, what could I do to recover? What was my action plan? Here's what I came up with.

I'd pound the pavement until I found another job—any job.

I'd live with family or friends until I got back on my feet (something I actually DID have to do).

I'd go to a shelter or find some other way to rebuild my life, no matter how hard it was or how long it took.

You know what? I could live with that.

Then I flipped the script and wrote down my best-case scenarios. I imagined all the potential benefits I might gain from moving forward. Here are some of the payoffs I imagined:

Joy and happiness from doing what I was born to do.

Fulfillment from making a positive difference to others.

Financial freedom.

The ability to take care of my family and friends.

Resources to give to others and causes I believe in.

A platform to support social change.

A chance to collaborate with people I admire.

Freedom to live anywhere I want.

Travel and adventure.

Nonstop learning, growth, and creativity.

Living regret-free.

Boom. Even if I experienced a fraction of that list, I'd die happy. While I knew absolutely nothing was guaranteed, the potential upside far outweighed my worst-case scenarios.

If you're legitimately afraid to move forward with an idea, take fifteen minutes to do this exercise now. Don't just think about it in your head. Articulate it on paper. Write down the *absolute worst* thing that could possibly happen and what that would mean to you—mentally, emotionally, and financially. Is it a matter of losing money? Shattering an ego or reputation? Could you lose your job or business? Disappoint family or loved ones? Ask yourself, "Okay. Now what's the worst thing possible if *that* happened?" Keep going until you get to the absolute worst thing you can possibly imagine. The place where you hit rock bottom. Next, on a scale of one to ten—one being unlikely and ten being guaranteed—what's the probability of that very worst-case scenario actually happening? Then, write the exact steps you could take to get back on your feet.

This exercise helps us realize that even if it all implodes (again, highly unlikely—especially when you address potential problems in advance), there's always *something* we can do to lift ourselves back up.

Worst-case scenarios are often low-probability events. They're even less likely to happen if you strategize how to prevent them from happening, and how you'd deal with them if they did.

Once you've articulated your darkest fears and recovery plan on paper, flip your perspective. This time, write down the best-case scenarios. What are all the possible upsides that could come from moving ahead? Will you reignite your joy and passion? Learn and grow? Live without a nagging sense of regret? Positively impact others? Are there financial rewards? Creative gains? Relationship benefits? Certain freedoms that may only come if you take a risk and say yes? Write these down, too. Be as concrete and specific as possible.

Once you do this exercise, you'll be ready to either move forward with step one of your idea (which is all you need to focus on right now), or adjust your plan so that the absolute worst-case scenario and recovery plan is something you can live with. An adjustment might look like breaking an enormous dream down into more doable, achievable chunks. Instead of quitting your job to write the next Great American Novel, keep your job and write your first short story. Maybe you can do a small-scale test before taking a higher-stake risk (e.g., living and working abroad for three weeks instead of three years).

The point is this: do *not* allow your fears to stay amorphous. Face them on the page. Chances are, your biggest fears are little more than figureoutable paper tigers.

LEVERAGE THE ALCHEMY OF LANGUAGE

There is nothing either good or bad, but thinking makes it so.

William Shakespeare

Josh's dad was a renowned theoretical physicist who worked with Einstein (yes, *that* Einstein). When Josh was a boy, his dad would explain that, at the deepest level, everything in the universe was made of the same stuff. An oak tree, a sports car, a human hand—all things are composed of atoms and energy, vibrating at ever-changing frequencies.

Josh grew up to become an actor and alongside his work in TV, film, and theater, he founded Committed Impulse, which trains actors and speakers to create spontaneous and electric performances.

One of the most powerful lessons in Committed Impulse challenges the idea that there are such things as "good" and "bad" emotions. What if all supposedly "bad" emotions, including fear or nervousness or anxiety, are just atoms and energy vibrating at different frequencies that we've been taught to label as "bad"? For example, if you described the emotion you call fear as a pure bodily sensation, how would you do it? Maybe you'd report a fluttering in your stomach. Or a tightening of your chest. Or a heaviness in your heart. Where exactly would that fear be located—your neck, forehead, or big toe? What would be its color, shape, texture, or movement pattern?

Remove the negative story you tell yourself about what those sensations mean—are those sensations themselves that terrible? Have you ever allowed yourself to really feel those sensations without going into a mental drama about them? Sure, they might not feel pleasant, but are they so intolerable that it's worth abandoning your biggest dreams in order to occasionally not experience them, even for just a few moments?

Consider the following. Is it possible that the emotion you've previously labeled as "fear" might be another emotion altogether? Is it possible that the sensation you've assumed is "fear" could also be called anticipation, expectation, or perhaps even excitement?

Legend has it that when Bruce Springsteen is about to go onstage in stadiums full of screaming fans, the Boss feels a host of physical sensations in his body:

> Just before I go onstage my heart beats a little faster . . . my
> hands sweat a little . . . my legs go numb as if I'm getting pins
> and needles . . . and then I get a tight feeling in the pit of my
> stomach that starts to spin round and round . . . When I get all
> those feelings, I know I'm excited, pumped up and ready to go
> onstage.[1]

Fascinating, right? Springsteen interprets those body sensations as a sign of readiness, not a sign that he's afraid, anxious, or incompetent. He's *chosen* to believe that the vibrations and sensations in his physical vessel are telling him he's prepared to give his fans a legendary performance. He's *chosen* an interpretation that serves him.

Nothing has any meaning besides the meaning we give it. Whether we realize it or not, we assign a meaning to everything in our lives—every event, every interaction, and (yes) every sensation. Just for fun, try this Committed Impulse exercise. Choose a new name for the "fear" sensation that stops you most often. Rather than saying you're scared or nervous or anxious or terrified, name that body sensation something cute and harmless like "shooshie" or "nooney" or "jambly." As in:

I'm about to ask for a raise and I'm feeling so damn shooshie about it.
OMG, consumed with nooney right now—sending off my pitch to the editor!
Holy cow. I'm bursting with jambly! I'm about to get onstage and give my talk to five thousand people!

Yes, I know. This sounds ridiculous. Which is precisely why it works. Sometimes, we need to stop taking ourselves so seriously. A silly word like "shooshie" breaks the trance of terror we put ourselves in and helps us lighten up. As Catelyn Stark in *Game of Thrones* so wisely said, "Laughter is poison to fear."

To be clear, relabeling your emotions doesn't mean denying them, suppressing them, or pretending they don't exist. You're still experiencing your physical sensations. You're breathing and present. You're feeling what you feel. You're metabolizing the energy inside you.

You're just not assigning what you feel a negative label or dramatic interpretation that hurts you rather than helps you. Emotions are just energy, and all energy can be transformed. Be like the Boss. Practice interpreting sweaty palms and a swirling, whirling stomach not as signs that you're afraid but as signs that you're ready to rock.

FEAR VS. INTUITION: HOW TO TELL THE DIFFERENCE

There is more wisdom in your body than in your deepest philosophy.

Friedrich Nietzsche

When you're faced with an opportunity to grow, it's normal to feel hesitant and unsure. But how do you tell the difference between helpful, directive fear that needs to be metabolized and moved through, and your intuition trying to tell you *not* to do something that you'll later regret?

This is an important distinction. I run my business and life by trusting my intuition. It's never steered me wrong. When those gut-based alarm bells go off, it's for good reason.

Whenever I feel torn about a situation and can't immediately tell whether I'm experiencing normal, healthy, directive fear (a sign to say yes and GROW!) or an intuitive hit to run the other way, I always find my answer through a subtle, visceral body check. This only takes seconds and it produces a clear answer. Every. Single. Time.

Here's how it works. Get in a comfortable seated or standing position. Close your eyes. Take a few deep, full breaths (at least three) and allow your mind to settle. Be present in your body. Then ask yourself the following question and pay careful attention to your instant, involuntary interior body reaction:

Does saying yes to this make me feel
expansive or contracted?

In other words, when you imagine moving ahead with this opportunity, what happens in your body the nanosecond after you ask that question? Do you feel an openness, a sense of moving forward, a lightness in your chest? Joy, excitement, or fun?

Or do you feel an immediate sense of heaviness and dread? Does your heart sink? Do you detect a tightening in your chest or a sick feeling in your tummy? Does something subtle inside of you retreat, pull back, close down, shut off, or somehow energetically say *no*—even though declining may not make logical sense?

I'm not talking about your thoughts. I'm not interested in what your mind thinks you "should" do. I'm asking you to pay attention to the truth and wisdom in your body. In your heart. When you pay close attention and listen to your nonverbal, almost preverbal cues—you'll notice a predominance of energy moving in one direction or the other. Obviously, if you feel anything close to expansive, joyful, or excited, that's intuition signaling to move ahead and say yes. Contraction, or any sense of dread, means it's a no-go.

Your body has innate wisdom that extends far beyond reason and logic. You can't think your way into accessing your body's intelligence, you have to feel your way in. Your heart, gut, intuition—whatever you want to call it—is far more intelligent than your mind. In a sedentary, screen-focused culture that normalizes living from the neck up, feeling and "hearing" what your body communicates takes practice. But like any other skill, it can be developed.

To gain better control over distinguishing between your fear and intuition, the following questions can help. Remember, the wisdom is in your body. Direct your attention inward as you answer these questions.

- Do I really *want* to do this?
- Do I feel expansive or contracted when I imagine saying yes to this?
- Does saying yes make me feel delight or dread?
- Does this feel joyful and fun?
- If I had $20 million sitting in the bank, would I still do this?
- When I'm around this person (or organization or environment), do I feel more confident and capable, or do I compare myself and feel "less than"?
- After I'm around this person, do I feel more energized or less energized?
- Do I trust them?
- Do I feel safe, understood, and respected?

Notice the first thing you feel or blurt out, even if it surprises you.

THE TRUTH ABOUT FAILURE

Once in an interview I was asked about my biggest failures. I choked. Froze like a deer in headlights. I had nothing. After, I felt weird and shitty about it. *Why couldn't I answer that simple question? It's not like I never make mistakes—I make them all the time!*

Then it hit me. There's no permanent failure folder in the file cabinet of my mind. Before you hate me or think I'm a special-snowflake-asshole life coach, let me explain. The reason I don't have that folder in my head anymore is because of an old adage I heard in my early twenties:

I win or I learn, but I never lose.

Immediately, it became one of my go-to mantras. Hearing it completely shifted my perspective. And thank God it did, because I used to love cataloging my mistakes. But the truth is, there's not one instance in my past where my supposed "wrong" action or "botched" attempt didn't eventually lead to something good and useful.

That's why I stumbled over that interview question. When I look back on this breathtaking, heartbreaking adventure called life, I legitimately don't see failures. Every painful misstep I've made has been a stepping-stone to a better me.

Now let's be real. In the midst of or immediately following a mess-up, do I sometimes cry and feel like a clueless idiot? Yes. Do I beat myself up if I wasted massive amounts of time, money, or energy? Yes, yes, and yes. But the nanosecond I remember "I win or I learn, but I never lose," I begin to regain sanity and perspective. Something good will (eventually) come out of this shitstorm. Something that'll help me grow and do better next time.

Failure as a concept is incredibly shortsighted. It's like watching a movie and stopping in the middle because the characters hit conflict. You have no clue where the story ends unless you keep going. This is true on the big screen and true for the ever-unfolding adventure of your life. Unless you're dead and reading this from the other side, you have *no* idea where this is all heading.

Right now, think about your past failures—projects that went nowhere, or times you crashed and burned. Relationships that took an unexpected left turn. Words, actions, or decisions that blew up. As painful as those memories may be, isn't it also true that, in the process, you learned something? Didn't you gain insight, understanding, or valuable experience? Haven't some of your setbacks or failures actually been re-directs that guided you to a higher path?

One of the best insights on failure came from a *MarieTV* guest, Judge Victoria Pratt. Judge Pratt gained international acclaim for her work reforming the criminal justice system in Newark, New Jersey. Instead of prison sentences, she handed out introspective essay assignments. Her courtroom had so much applause that it was compared to an off-Broadway show. Judge Pratt said to me:

> **"Failure is just an event. It is not a characteristic.**
> **People can't be failures."**

Let that sink in. *People can't be failures.* Look. We all make shitty judgment calls. But your flops are events, not permanent character traits. Failure is not who you are.

YOU are not a failure and can never be one.

Think about the word "FAIL" like this: it's a faithful attempt in learning. That's it. A faithful attempt in *learning.* It's nothing to fear and nothing to avoid. From this perspective, failure is not a glitch in your figureoutable journey, it's a must-have feature. As cliché as it sounds, you can only truly fail if you stop learning and growing.

INSIGHT TO ACTION
CHALLENGE

You gain strength, courage, and confidence by every experience in which you really stop to look fear in the face.

Eleanor Roosevelt

1. ***What's the worst-worst-worst-case scenario you imagine could
   happen if you moved ahead on your idea?*** Is it losing money?
   Looking stupid? Could you lose your job or business? Disappoint
   family or loved ones? Your goal is to brain dump and get your deepest fears out of your head and onto the page. Keep going until you hit
   your fear's rock bottom. Then ask yourself, "Okay. So what's the worst
   thing possible if *that* happened?" Push yourself until you get to the
   basement of your fear.

2. ***Take a look at what you've written.*** How likely do you think it is
   that this full-blown nightmare will occur? On a scale from one to
   ten—one being not at all likely and ten being guaranteed—how
   probable is this?

3. ***Now write out the exact steps you'd take to recover and rebuild*** if
   the worst of the worst did in fact happen. If you had to, how would
   you get back on your feet?

4. *Flip the script.* What's the best-case scenario? What are all the possible payoffs—the upsides—that could come from moving ahead? Write down as many as you can.

5. *Explore fear as your GPS.* Get curious and listen to your fear. What helpful, positive signal might fear be sending? What productive message is she attempting to communicate? What is she directing you toward?

6. *Leverage your language.* If saying that you feel terrified, stressed, afraid, anxious, or nervous tends to get you frozen or overwhelmed, rename it. Borrow "shooshie" or "nooney," or come up with your own new word. (Hint: Strive for something that sounds ridiculous.)

7. *Think about a specific time you "failed" (or more accurately, made a faithful attempt in learning).* Mine the gold from it. What are three good things that came from it? What lessons did you learn? What valuable understanding do you now have that you wouldn't have otherwise?

Bonus Material

Fear is a sprawling subject. We've got dozens of free *MarieTV* episodes and podcasts that touch upon all flavors of fear including: the fear of success, the fear of public speaking, the fear of money, the fear of self-promotion, the fear of being a fraud, the fear that you're just not good enough, etc. Find them at MarieForleo.com/MarieTV.

Figureoutable Field Notes

She used everything is figureoutable *to leave an abusive relationship—with two kids and no backup plan. She broke a toxic cycle and is rebuilding her life, one smart step at a time.*

I left my abusive marriage after twenty years. Honestly, Marie, I was psychologically paralyzed during this marriage. The level of abuse brought me to the point where I believed I simply was not strong enough to leave.

Your calm approach to chaos is one of the main concepts that allowed me to know that, while I didn't know what was on the other side of leaving, I knew I could "figure it out." With my two children in tow, I left with their keepsakes, my education, my career, my dignity, and my dying car. I am figuring it out, one day at a time. And now my children are witnessing how to break a toxic cycle.

Thank you, Marie. Truly, everything is figureoutable. Even the things I believed were impossible. Listening to you, and how you approach life, made me see that I could take one step (in this case, a plan to be financially stable on my own), and then another (obtaining a competent attorney and an escape plan). Then, I took action.

The end result is that I'm away from that horrible situation, my children are on a better path to understanding that preserving one's sense of self and integrity far outweighs the public perception of perfection, and I am now building a solid reputation in my career.

—JESSICA
MISSOURI

6

Define Your Dream

Everything's in the mind. That's where it all starts. Knowing what you want is the first step toward getting it.

Mae West

Do you remember when you were little and adults repeatedly asked, "What do you want to be when you grow up?" I could never name one thing.

I want to be a writer and an artist and a dancer and a businesswoman and an animator and a teacher and a singer and a fashion designer and and and . . . a makeup artist!

That list morphed throughout school, but it was always long as hell. I assumed all my interests would magically merge through the alchemy of college and I'd graduate with a singular thing "to be." That's not quite how it went.

I was in my midtwenties and feeling like the most pathetic life coach on the planet. I'd recently broken off an engagement to a sweet but wrong-for-me guy, which left me emotionally raw, broke, and without a place to live. Desperate, I moved back in with my parents in New Jersey to get back on my feet. (Yes, my folks divorced when I was eight but reconciled several years later.)

After my second week at their house, Mom and I had a major blow-out. It was painfully clear I couldn't stay there any longer. Mercifully, a generous friend from my magazine days was willing to take me in. I slept on an air mattress in the living room of her tiny and charming West Village apartment. She was an angel for letting me crash with her. (Thank you, Dana.)

So there I was, a struggling life coach feeling like the biggest loser. Evenings were spent slinging drinks and waiting tables while I worked on my business during the day. But I couldn't shake this unrelenting feeling that my life was passing by *so* fast and I was nowhere near where I thought I should be by now.

As much as I loved coaching and personal development, something still felt slightly incomplete. Like there was a missing piece (or several) to my work-life puzzle. Deep down, I believed I had *something* unique to give to the world. But I still felt like an unaccomplished misfit.

I dreaded people asking me, "So what do *you* do?" The shame made me want to crawl out of my skin. Plus, calling myself a "life coach" and focusing only on that profession felt narrow and limiting. I couldn't deny a desire to explore other aspects of my creativity—like hip-hop dance, fitness, and writing. I was also über-passionate about the embryonic world of online business and digital media. (Remember, this was around 2002.) My journals from those days were filled with desperate pleas to God.

Why can't I just pick one thing to focus on like everyone else?

What's wrong with me?

How do I know that life coaching is the only thing I'm supposed to do with my life?

What if I'm wasting my other talents and gifts? None of this feels right!

Is there something wrong with my brain? Am I just not able to focus?

Am I just broken?

Professionally, I was all over the place. I loved coaching, but I couldn't see myself doing *only* that. In my hunt for answers, I started reading every classic book on career, business, and success I could find. Most of them offered different versions of the same conventional advice:

"Dominate a niche."

"The more specialized you are, the more quickly you'll succeed."

Intellectually, that advice made sense. But every time I tried to "choose one thing"—like coaching or even a singular aspect of coaching—it felt like I was cutting off a limb. A little voice inside of me kept nudging . . . *You're MORE than just one thing, Marie—stop trying to fit in.*

The most intense and immediate pull I felt was toward dance and fitness. The problem was, I had no formal training in either. Sure, in my teens, I was obsessed with a TV show called *Bodies in Motion* with a hunky Israeli-born trainer named Gilad (pronounced Gih-LAHD). Before long, I started designing my own workouts and became a proud, iron-pumping member of Gold's Gym.

When it came to dance, I did moonwalk across my mom's linoleum floor. I picked up moves from shows like *Yo! MTV Raps* and *Club MTV* with Downtown Julie Brown. I even won teen dance contests at the local under-eighteen night clubs in Seaside Heights, New Jersey. The passion was always there, but I had never once stepped foot in an actual class. I had zero technique and zero clue how to enter the dance world at age twenty-five, which, sadly, is considered "old" for a newbie.

Exasperation produced my first breakthrough. Since the traditional career advice to choose one thing made me want to slam my head against the wall, I finally said, *Fuck it. I'm done trying to fit in. I'm in a ton of debt. I'm living on an air mattress. Why not experiment? What do I have to lose?**

New York City is home to the legendary Broadway Dance Center (BDC). If I was going to take my first real dance class, I might as well go to the pros.

To be clear, I was terrified. I had horrible visions of tripping over my feet and bumping into people left and right. I imagined being laughed at, booed, and shooed out the door. Plus, I was nearly a decade older than other students, all of whom I imagined had been taking dance classes since popping out of the womb.

I pushed myself anyway and signed up for Absolute Beginner Modern Jazz. I was wearing the crappiest, dorkiest outfit. Lurking outside the studio, I watched the previous class finish their routine. Everyone was *so* talented. They were *so* cool. *So* young.

Once the previous class filtered out, I slunk in and tried to stay invisible. Other students filed in and sat down. *Oh, I guess we start by sitting.* The teacher walked in, didn't say a word or acknowledge anyone. There were a few moments of total silence before a loud, deep, steady bass beat filled the room. The music jolted every cell in my body. Everyone

---

*Fuck-it moments: noun; when you stop trying to look good, stop trying to fit in, and finally follow your heart. Usually huge, positive turning points.

(besides me) began moving and stretching in sync. They understood exactly when to progress to the next stretch by a hand clap from the teacher.

Less than seven seconds after the music started, I burst into tears. I didn't know what the hell was happening or why, but I couldn't stop. I sat there trying to keep up as I sobbed uncontrollably. I covered my face with my hair and thanked sweet Jesus the music was loud enough that no one could hear me. That dance floor felt like home. *YASSS!!!* my body screamed as I moved. *FINALLY. You're listening.*

I'm still shocked at how much time and energy we humans can waste being indecisive, talking about ideas (in our heads or aloud) but never doing anything about them. I spent years wondering if I had what it took to be a dancer. *Could I be one? Should I be one?* I even fantasized about what it might be like. But I never made a move, until I did. My biggest mistake? Searching my head for an answer that could only be experienced through my heart. That's when I learned a lesson I still live by to this day:

Clarity comes from engagement, not thought.

Write that down. Memorize it. Tattoo it on your tush. Whenever you're trapped in the hell of indecision, do something about it as quickly as possible. Find a way to take a tangible, real action and you'll be rewarded with priceless feedback to inform your next steps.

Wondering for the seventy-fifth time whether to break up with your partner? *Take time apart, even if it's just a few days. Even if it means sleeping on someone's couch. Find a damn good couple's therapist and either commit to heal or commit to move on. ENGAGE.*

Can't stop thinking about changing careers? *Take a class. Secure an internship (no matter your age). Work for free on weekends. Whatever it takes, experience the industry firsthand. ENGAGE.*

Fantasizing about moving to a new state or even country? *Research. Figure out how much it will cost you to move and how you can make a living there. Make a short trip to feel the place out. ENGAGE.*

Can't pick the right glass of wine at dinner? *Ask your server for just a sip of your top two choices. They rarely say no. ENGAGE and SALUTE!*

When you're stuck in a paralyzing thought loop of indecision, stop thinking and start doing. Make a move, no matter how tiny. Find (or make) a way to do a real-world experiment. Action is the fastest and most direct route to clarity.

DECIDING WHAT YOU WANT IS THE FIRST STEP TO GETTING IT

> Discovering what you really want saves you endless confusion and wasted energy.
>
> *Stuart Wilde*

Whenever I work one-on-one with people, during our initial session I say, "I can help you get anything you want, but first you have to tell me what that is." Sounds simple. But simple doesn't always mean easy.

How many of us are crystal clear about what we're working to create? Can we honestly say, "THIS. This _____ [idea, relationship, project, film, book, cause, startup, skill, healing journey, habit, goal, etc.] is the main focus of my life right now. This is what I'm willing to work days, nights, and weekends to make happen, no matter what it takes."

When I've been unclear about my primary focus or, worse, too afraid to admit what I want, suffering always ensues. Headaches and heartaches all around. Ignoring our truth doesn't make it go away, it only spawns despair and dysfunction.

When you don't have something clear and meaningful to work toward, you can experience a host of other problems:

- Feeling lost, not where you should be by now, and off track. You have recurring thoughts like, *Is this all there is? Am I really doing what I'm supposed to be doing in life?*
- Struggling to prioritize or schedule your time because you don't know what's most important or how to navigate competing opportunities.
- Failing to produce meaningful results, despite always being "super busy." You confuse activity with accomplishment: *I'm running myself ragged, but I have nothing substantial to show for it.*
- Teetering on the edge of burnout. You're exhausted and irritated, and you fantasize about running away and never looking back.

The struggle is real, but it's also understandable. I never took a Dream Clarity Class, did you? Most of us have little-to-no instruction on how to figure out what we really want in life. Or how to get back on track when we've lost our way.

In this hands-on chapter, you'll name and claim what you most want to figure out—your most exciting dream, goal, project, or life change. If you already know your answer, fantastic. What follows will strengthen your resolve and motivation as we move ahead. If you're drawing a blank or are afraid to admit what you really want, these action challenges are crucial.

I won't lie, this work can be tough. But the more difficult it is, the more you need it. The clearer you are about what you want to figure out, the better chance you have of actually doing it. Clarity equals power.

At this stage, all you need is an initial destination—something meaningful that challenges you to learn and grow. You don't need an epic world-changing goal, especially if that feels overwhelming. You also don't need to know *how* you'll make this dream happen. You just need a clear mark, because you can't hit a target you can't see.

Here's what's exciting about this process. Once you clarify and commit to a dream, mysterious forces begin to stir that would otherwise remain inert. Powerful, miraculous forces that are both cosmic and scientific in nature. William Hutchison Murray, a Scottish mountaineer, best articulates the former in his 1951 book *The Scottish Himalayan Expedition*:

> Until one is committed there is hesitancy, the chance to draw back, always ineffectiveness. Concerning all acts of initiative (and creation), there is one elementary truth, the ignorance of which kills countless ideas and splendid plans: that the moment one definitely commits oneself, then Providence moves too. . . . A whole stream of events issues from the decision, raising in one's favour all manner of unforeseen incidents and meetings and material assistance, which no man could have dreamt would have come his way.

We live in a highly intelligent and responsive universe. Whether you're aware of the process or not, you're co-creating your reality through the thoughts, words, and behaviors you choose minute by minute, hour by hour, day by day. Your life is an ongoing act of creation and you're 100 percent in charge. When you make a clear, committed decision about something you want, it's analogous to picking up the phone and placing a to-go order with the cosmos. That's why, as much as possible, you must strive to be decisive, clear, and specific. Wishy-washy goals get wishy-washy results.

One of the primary reasons people don't get what they want is they're afraid to ask for it. They're frightened they don't have what it takes. But here's a secret that many people miss:

You wouldn't have the dream if you didn't already have what it takes to make it happen.

You were born with everything you need to answer the call of your soul. That call encompasses the vast realm of intuitive desires, creative projects, ideas, goals, and dreams you hold in your heart.

BEING TRUE TO YOURSELF AND YOUR DREAMS

Our creative dreams and yearnings come from a divine source. As we move towards our dreams, we move towards our divinity.

Julia Cameron

As a young child raised by a single mom in Mobile, Alabama, Laverne Cox was bullied daily. She was chased home from school by kids who wanted to beat her up because she didn't act like a child who was assigned male at birth was supposed to act.

In third grade, after falling in love with a gorgeous peacock fan during a field trip,[1] her teacher called her mom and said, "Your son is going to end up in New Orleans wearing a dress if you don't get him into therapy right away."[2] That moment, Laverne says, was "profoundly shaming."[3]

The therapist suggested giving Laverne testosterone shots to "fix" her.[4] Finding that completely unacceptable, her mom pulled her out of therapy right away. In a 2015 interview with the *Telegraph*, Laverne shared, "As a child I knew everyone was telling me that I was a boy but I felt like a girl. I thought I would hit puberty and just start turning into a girl."[5]

In sixth grade—right around the time she started feeling attracted to boys—Laverne swallowed a bottle of pills because she didn't want to be herself anymore and she didn't know how to be anybody else. Who she was, she was told, was a "sin" and a "problem." She didn't want to exist.[6]

What she did want was to perform. She begged her mother for classes, but they couldn't afford it. Then her mom discovered an arts program for disadvantaged families. In her *Telegraph* interview, Laverne said, "Suddenly I had this creative outlet, I had something that I loved, and something that I could aspire to. When I think about my childhood and being happy, it was when I was dancing, being creative, performing and being onstage."

She eventually won a scholarship to the Alabama School of Fine Arts, where she began experimenting with dressing in women's clothes. While she was still bullied, she finally started becoming more comfortable with herself.

Like many aspiring performers, Laverne moved to New York with only a few dollars in her pocket. For the first time, Laverne was celebrated for who she was. In the New York club scene, looking unique was an advantage. "I was still getting harassed on the streets for how I looked," she said, "but at night I was a star."[7]

She took acting classes and was able to book a few gigs. To make ends meet she worked as a waitress and a performer in bars. It wasn't until 2007 that actress Candis Cayne became the first trans woman to have a recurring role on primetime TV. When that breakthrough happened Laverne said to herself, "This is the moment."[8]

Newly inspired, Laverne sent hundreds of postcards to casting directors and managers that read: "Laverne Cox is the solution to all your acting needs." Out of those five hundred mailings she got four meetings, and one of those meetings led to her manager.

Still, by May 2012, Laverne hadn't booked an acting job in almost a year. She thought about quitting and going to graduate school. She bought some GRE study materials from a friend and started looking into schools. But after taking a vacation with her mom and lugging those study books with her, she realized grad school just wasn't for her (clarity comes from engagement, not thought!). She recommitted herself to acting, and set a goal for herself to land a recurring role that year. That's when she got the call to audition for a Netflix original series.

Of course, if you've ever seen the wildly popular show *Orange Is the New Black*, then you know Laverne booked that gig. She later won two Emmys and became the first openly trans person to grace the cover of *Time* magazine. In interviews with *Metro Weekly*, Laverne shared:

> So many young trans people dream of being an actor and don't think it's possible because they're trans. There was a point where I almost gave up. Luckily, I didn't. . . . I don't like the term "role model," though. I prefer the term "possibility model."

To be clear, Laverne moved to New York in 1993 and shot *Orange Is the New Black* in 2012. That's nineteen years. Even though she came close, she never quit on her dream. In fact, from the moment she got the opportunity and a platform, she's used her voice to give back. "When I began to understand that it was my job to be of service, to use being trans as something that was not a deficit that would keep me from acting [but as] something that made me unique and special, my career changed," she said.[9]

From her acting to her activism, Laverne demonstrates the power that comes from staying fiercely true to yourself, and to your dreams.

RECRUITING YOUR RAS: YOUR WISH IS ITS COMMAND

If you are possessed by an idea, you find it expressed everywhere, you even *smell* it.

Thomas Mann

What if I told you that you have a magical neurological genie working 24/7/365 to guide and support you? Here's how being clear and specific about what you want supercharges your brain's ability to help you figure out how to get it.

Your brain is bombarded with billions of bits of information every second of every day. Unsurprisingly, it doesn't consciously process it all, but despite the constant flood of data, your brain also doesn't short-circuit either. Why is that? How does your brain decide what to let in and what to disregard? Part of the answer lies in a complex neural network called the reticular activating system (RAS). Among other crucial functions, your RAS acts as an attention filter. It automatically sifts and sorts incoming data, filtering out what's unimportant from your conscious awareness and allowing through only what is important. Your RAS is the reason you can often tune out the din of a noisy café but instantly snap to if you hear someone call your name. It's the reason you never noticed or cared about "dry brushing" until a friend said it was THE thing that transformed her skin. All of a sudden, tips, articles, and conversations about dry brushing appear and occur nonstop.

In his book *The Organized Mind,* author Daniel J. Levitin writes:

> Millions of neurons are constantly monitoring the environment to select the most important things for us to focus on. These neurons are collectively the *attentional filter.* They work largely in the background, outside of our conscious awareness. This is why most of the perceptual detritus of our daily lives doesn't register, or why, when you've been driving on the freeway for several hours at a stretch, you don't remember much of the scenery that has whizzed by: Your attentional system "protects" you from registering it because it isn't deemed important.

The act of clearly defining your dream will tell your brain that this *thing* is now valuable and should take priority. You'll recruit your RAS to help you bring this dream to life. Your RAS will begin scanning your environment for any and all opportunities, people, and information related to what you've declared a significant goal. It'll begin processing, culling ideas, and directing you to pay attention to solutions you need, whether you're fully aware of it or not.

How do you think this book got in your hands? This material just didn't appear by accident. Some deeper, wiser part of you led you to these very words. Your RAS is already doing its job. It's working to help make the change some part of you is aching to make.

Stay on the lookout. Keep your eyes, ears, and heart open. An insight may be revealed in the next song you hear on the radio. Or through a story line you see in a movie this weekend. Or in an article you stumble upon online. Maybe a chance encounter with a stranger at the grocery store will guide your next step. Or you'll receive a flash of creative intuition in the shower or on your commute. The point is this: once you cognitively and emotionally identify an important target, your RAS will work nonstop to accomplish the mission. No matter how long it takes, or how unpredictable your path becomes, it will diligently and persistently stay on task. Day in and day out, it'll sort through masses of data and information, guiding you toward exactly what you need to see, hear, or pay attention to next.

See? You do have a powerful genie inside your mind working her magical buns off to help you achieve what you want. Her only requirement is that you clearly state your wish.

HOW TO INCREASE YOUR ODDS OF SUCCESS BY 42 PERCENT

Going back through old journals and notebooks can be eye-opening. I've written down endless thoughts, dreams, and fragments of ideas that, at the time, seemed ridiculous. In the early years of my fledgling business, I devoured information about iconic entrepreneurs. I came across the work of Sir Richard Branson and his nonprofit, Virgin Unite, and was captivated. I loved the irreverent nature of this highly successful for-profit brand coupled with a fierce commitment to philanthropy through their nonprofit arm. I scribbled "Virgin Unite" on a yellow legal pad and forgot about it.

A whopping *nine* years later, I met someone from Virgin Unite at an event in New York. That chance encounter led to an invitation to mentor local startups in South Africa . . . and spend time with Sir Richard Branson himself. I wound up doing several more projects with Virgin Unite and developed a wonderful relationship with the team. It wasn't until many years later, while cleaning out an old cabinet, that I found that yellow legal pad with "Virgin Unite" scribbled on it. That's just one example of an idea that seemed wildly unlikely at the time, but years later had come to fruition in ways I never expected.

This isn't surprising. An oft-cited study done by Dr. Gail Matthews, a psychology professor at Dominican University of California, shows that you're 42 percent more likely to achieve your goals if you write them down. Gail's sample group included men and women, ages twenty-three to seventy-two, from around the world and all walks of life—entrepreneurs, educators, health care professionals, artists, lawyers, and bankers. She divided the participants into two groups, those who wrote down their goals and those who didn't. The results were clear. Those who wrote down their goals achieved those desires at a significantly higher level than those who didn't.

As basic as it seems, most people still don't write down what's most important to them. If I was considering making a bet and you told me that if I wrote that bet on paper, I had a 42 percent HIGHER chance of winning—I'd do it! If I was undergoing some kind of medical protocol and my doctor said, "Hey, if you write this down, you'll increase your chances of healing by 42 percent"—am I NOT going to listen? Who doesn't want those kind of odds?

Even without this study, writing down what you want is sheer common sense. In our endlessly distracted, overcommitted, overstretched world, writing down what's most important is a deceptively easy way to stay focused. Writing down your dream forces you to be clear and specific about what you want. Ambiguity is the enemy of accomplishment.

Not to mention it's what we naturally do in every other area of life when we want to produce a result. If you're renovating your kitchen, you don't just wake up and take a sledgehammer to the sink. You design a plan on paper first. Need to pick up groceries from the supermarket? Write a list. Want to master a new subject? Take written notes. Going on a trip? Map out your destination. Think about any professional project you've been a part of. Contracts, work agreements, and purchase orders turn everyday ideas into reality. No matter what you want to figure out, one thing is for sure: writing it down is a fundamental step to making it real.

Now, obviously, you shouldn't just write your goal in a journal and call it a day. You should look at it often. Daily is ideal. This keeps your top priority top of mind.

INSIGHT TO ACTION
CHALLENGE

This action challenge is longer and more in depth than previous ones. Strap yourself in and pull down your lap bar. We're going on a ride into the deepest recesses of your heart and soul. I promise, the focus, honesty, and effort you put in right now will pay off tenfold.

STEP 1: LIST YOUR TOP
ONE-YEAR DREAMS

A dream is a wish your heart makes.
Cinderella *(1950 film)*

Set a timer for fifteen minutes and make a list of the top dreams, goals, or projects you're most excited **to start figuring out within the next year.** These can be painful problems you need to solve or aspirations you're ready to materialize. Write down anything that comes to mind that you'd like to change, start, stop, pursue, heal, transform, learn, experience, explore, become, create, or achieve.

IMPORTANT NOTE: It's not necessary that you accomplish this dream within the year, but **it's imperative that you're willing to start now.** If you're clear on exactly what you want to figure out, you can either brainstorm a list of one-year dreams for fun (your answers might surprise you!), or move straight to the next step.

If you're already feeling anxious because you can't come up with anything, don't worry. Not knowing what you want is more common than you might think. Some of us have been pleasing others and suppressing our own dreams for so long we've lost touch with our own desires. These questions help. Use as many of these prompts as you like.

- If you could wave a magic wand and change *one* thing about your life or the world, what would it be?
- What breaks your heart about life, work, or the world?
- What pisses you off about life, work, or the world?
- If you had two extra hours a day, what would you do with that time?
- Finish this sentence: *Wouldn't it be cool if* . . . For example:

Wouldn't it be cool if . . .

- *I stopped working on Fridays*
- *My partner and I had more sex*
- *Girls around the world had access to education*
- *I could find the perfect executive assistant*
- *I could speak fluent Spanish*
- *Prescription drugs were less expensive*
- *I had a six-month emergency fund*
- *I lived in Florence for the summer*
- *I turned my side hustle into a full-time job*
- *I found an extra hour each day to work on my book*
- *Every human had access to clean water*
- *I loved my body and felt strong in my skin*
- *I didn't feel so helpless and alone all the time*

You get the idea.

So you know, this last "Wouldn't it be cool if . . ." prompt is magic. We do this exercise regularly in my company. It's consistently produced multimillion-dollar breakthroughs. It started years ago when my business was much smaller and our team retreats took place in my living room. We sat in a circle on the floor brainstorming creative ideas for where and how to grow the business. One by one, each person finished the sentence "Wouldn't it be cool if . . ." and threw out their own crazy, exciting, OMG-could-we-really-do-that project.

Often, just saying these dreams out loud would make us scream with delight and expand our landscape of possibilities. We'd know we stumbled upon a winning idea when, all of a sudden, the room fell silent and we all had goosebumps. One big rule: When you're in "Wouldn't it be cool if . . ." brainstorming mode, no idea is too outlandish.

Most important, when you're brainstorming, be brutally honest about what you want. Don't censor or edit yourself. Don't write things you *should* want. Don't write dreams out of guilt or obligation. And don't try to write perfectly. The gold in brainstorming often comes much later in the process. Your responses are for your eyes only. If you're still drawing a blank or having trouble finding anything that you really want, go to the Define Your Dream FAQ section later in this chapter for a more in-depth dream-excavating exercise.

STEP 2: GET REAL ABOUT THIS DREAM

> He who has a *why* to live for can bear with almost
> any *how*.
>
> *Viktor E. Frankl*

Look back at your list. There's likely one or two items that make your heart jump with fear or excitement (or both!). Select the one you feel most drawn to, circle it, and answer the questions below.

The purpose of this step is to give yourself a reality check. How important is this dream to you right now? If you're torn between several dreams, complete all questions for dream number one, then repeat all questions for dream number two, and so on. Be ruthless in your responses, especially with this first section. Your answers may range from the superficial (*Why? Because I want to be rich and famous*) to the super moving (*Why? Because I want to make sure every girl has access to the education she deserves*). Get it all down on the page. Remember, no one needs to see this but you.

A. Importance: Why is this dream important to you? What difference will this make in your life once you figure it out? How will it impact you creatively, emotionally, physically, and financially? **Who else will be positively impacted by you figuring this out?** List as many whys as you can. Then, for every why you generate, dig deeper. Ask yourself, "And why is *that* important?" Then ask it again: "And why is *that* important?" "What will *that* ultimately do for me and others?" Drill down several layers until you get to the core of why this dream matters and what you want to feel, experience, or share as a result of achieving it. Do *not* skip this step. Purpose fuels persistence. Reasons come before results. If you don't have a stack of heart-based, compelling, true-to-you reasons why this must get figured out, it won't.

Given what you uncovered above, how important is this for you to start figuring out now?

1 = Tragically unimportant. 10 = Must take action NOW!

1   2   3   4   5   6   7   8   9   10

Obviously, we want a ten. Anything less than a seven should give you pause. If it's below a five, STOP. Go back to your brainstorm list and find something that's a must for you to start now.

B. Difficulty: Take a look at your dream and ask yourself, has anyone in the history of the world already figured this out? Chances are, yes. The vast majority of our dreams have been done before. If not exactly, something close enough. For example, living debt-free, winning a Grammy, running a profitable business, learning to do a headstand, making a living through your art, enjoying a loving long-term marriage, forgiving abuse/assault/murder, opening a restaurant, curing smallpox, launching a sustainable nonprofit, changing the laws to favor equality, walking on the moon, building schools in impoverished countries, developing disruptive technologies from a garage—these are all things that have been done by human beings throughout history. And they all started with at least one person figuring something out. If they did it, so can you.

Right now, ask yourself on a scale of one to ten, with one being "many people have done this" and ten being "no one in the entire history of the earth has ever done anything like this and it will likely be hard as hell," where does your dream fall?

1   2   3   4   5   6   7   8   9   10

If hundreds, thousands, or even millions of people have done what you want to do or something analogous to it, don't reinvent the wheel or cry in a corner about how hard it is.

Everything worthwhile is hard. Excruciatingly hard.

Embrace that fact. Respect it. You're about to work your ass off for this. Find a way to derive pleasure, however perverse that seems, out of doing hard, meaningful things. It builds strength and character. Plus, crushing an "impossible" dream is addictive as hell.

A lower difficulty rating can help you save time by learning from others. It can also mitigate unnecessary meltdowns. A higher score can help you prepare mentally and emotionally for a more difficult and vigorous journey ahead. In any case, understanding more about the level of difficulty you've chosen (and how others have fared before you) allows you to protect yourself from the inevitable minefields of frustration that lie ahead.

C. Past Attempts: Have you attempted this dream before and fallen short? If so, what went wrong? Don't beat yourself up. Be as objective as possible. Consider whatever you discover as positive news. If you've been the problem, that means you're also the solution. Write down exactly what didn't work and what you'll do differently to solve for those issues in advance. A moment of self-reflection can prevent repeating costly mistakes that have foiled past efforts.

STEP 3: CHOOSE ONE

If you run after two hares, you catch neither.
Proverb

It's time to make your choice. It's essential that you choose just one significant dream for now. Not seven. Not three. *One.*

This dream will serve as your training ground to master the figure-outable philosophy. You must develop your ability to focus and concentrate. In doing so, you'll cultivate a set of mental strengths, emotional disciplines, and behavioral habits that'll help you accomplish all future goals. Please erase from your mind the notion that you can figure out several significant dreams at the same time. Trying to multitask at this stage is a recipe for frustration and failure. It's like deciding to run three ultra marathons, back-to-back, with zero training.

You know this. Significant dreams come with significant challenges. If this dream is important, the road ahead won't be filled with rainbows and unicorns. You must build tolerance and strengthen your ability to move through the emotions that accompany this kind of journey. Emotions like panic, frustration, discomfort, insecurity, and impatience (you know, the fun ones). This is why it's imperative you choose *one* primary dream—for now. You'll need all of your prowess to conquer it.

Now don't get me wrong. You should continue to flex your figure-outable muscles as often as you can. Daily life supplies endless opportunities to train and practice. From fixing a running toilet to solving an unexpected shitshow at work to staying calm during a traffic jam, say, "Everything is figureoutable," and conquer problems head-on.

STEP 4: MAKE IT SPECIFIC, MEASURABLE, AND ACTIONABLE

> The secret of getting ahead is getting started. The secret of getting started is breaking your complex overwhelming tasks into small manageable tasks, and then starting on the first one.
>
> *Mark Twain*

Whether or not Mark Twain actually said that is debatable. Nevertheless, those words are The Truth. Every dream must be chunked down and clarified in order to get started. In this step, you must convert your dream into something specific, measurable, and actionable. For example:

"Get in shape" becomes "Be able to do twenty full-on push-ups within thirty days." Or if you want to form a habit of working out consistently, maybe something like this: "Get in shape" becomes "Work out five days a week for thirty minutes for the next thirty days no matter what."

"Find a new career" might become "Register for that photography workshop and find at least three local photographers to talk with by Sunday."

"Make more money" might become "Increase my net worth by paying off my credit card debt over the next eighteen months."

"Fix my marriage" might become "Interview at least three couples' therapists and read that *Getting the Love You Want* book within six weeks." (FYI, that book is *magic*.)

"Get sober" might become "Get to an AA meeting today."

"Be a great author" might become "Write for thirty minutes a day and finish a first draft of my book by Christmas."

State your dream in a way that you or anyone else could measure. This forces you to chunk your dream down and make it unmistakably actionable. The point here isn't to map out every single step. Instead, use simple, clear baby steps. They'll help cultivate a set of mental, emotional, and behavioral disciplines, which the following chapters address.

STEP 5: DETERMINE YOUR NEXT THREE STEPS AND GET STARTED NOW

> The most difficult thing is the decision to act. The rest is merely tenacity.
>
> *Amelia Earhart*

What are three simple actions you can take to get closer to that eventual goal of figuring it out? What could you do in ten minutes or less, the first of which could be done right now? Focus on small, active steps like making a phone call, setting up an appointment, sending an email, doing a push-up, or registering for a class. While I'm all for research, it's often an easy way to procrastinate and stay in your comfort zone. If you must research something, how can you make that research more hands-on? Instead of reading an article, find someone to talk with who's done what you want to do. Rather than watching an online tutorial, sign up for a local class. This isn't always possible, but train yourself to move toward discomfort. Put yourself in situations that feel scary and intimidating—that's where the figureoutable magic is!

As you'll discover in the next chapter, you must bypass your tendency to say, "Hold on a sec, I'm not quite *ready* yet."

No matter what, take that first action step today. I'm talking right NOW. Bookmark this page and go do your first step. Then add step two and three into your calendar, too.

I'll wait.

Because as the saying goes, someday is not a day of the week.

A WORD TO THE WISE: FOCUS ONLY ON WHAT YOU CAN CONTROL

> You can control two things: your work ethic and your attitude about anything.
>
> *Ali Krieger*

This simple idea is critical to your success.

Always direct the lion's share of your attention, energy, and effort to what you can control, not what you can't. Here's what's always in your control: your words, actions, behavior, attitude, perspective, focus, effort, and energy. You're also in control of how you respond to events and circumstances as they occur, whether you like them or not.

Here's what's never within your control: other people and their words, actions, behavior, attitude, perspective, focus, effort, and energy. You also can't control the weather, acts of God, or natural laws that govern our existence (e.g., gravity).

Let's say your dream involves securing a new job. While you're not able to make someone hire you (that's out of your control), the most crucial factors that determine your success are 100 percent within your control. Just a few include:

- How often and how many positions you apply for
- Making your résumé as competitive as possible
- Getting referrals and letters of recommendation
- Strengthening your interview skills
- The depth of the research and preparation you do on the company, team, and position
- How you show up, including punctuality, energy, attitude, and communication skills
- How effectively you demonstrate the value you'll bring to the company
- Thank-you notes, timely communication, and proper follow-up
- Whether you ask for feedback to learn and improve
- Whether you get better or bitter with each challenge or rejection
- Whether you consider remote work or moving to a new location
- The persistence to keep growing and going until you find a position

At some point, all dreams require cooperation, buy-in, or at the very least harmonious interactions with others. Make a lifelong commitment to cultivating social intelligence. That includes learnable disciplines like the art of persuasion, influence, marketing, and sales—even if you don't think you need those skills. Because you do. Each of those are meaty and deep areas of study, with volumes of existing literature just waiting to be devoured. While you can't change or control others, you can ethically and masterfully learn how to communicate in a way that increases your chances of getting a yes.

From this moment forward, no matter what you're figuring out, focus on what you can control, not what you can't. For bonus points, take a look at your dream and write your responses to the following questions:

What parts of this process are within my control?
What skills do I need to develop and master?

Your answers will provide endless inspiration for the next action steps.

DEFINE YOUR DREAM FAQS

Q: But what if I have many goals, dreams, and projects I want to accomplish this year?

A: That's wonderful. Write them all down. To get the most benefit from this book, and to master the *everything is figureoutable* approach to life, it's crucial that you focus on one primary goal. Choose the one that's most pressing, inspiring, and important. The one you're obsessed with. The one that causes the most pain, fear, or excitement. My intention is to get you results for life. For that to happen, you must develop discipline, focus, and a bias toward action. You must internalize the habits, perspectives, and mental models that get you to the figureoutable finish line. Choose one significant goal and slay that sucker. Then by all means: lather, rinse, and repeat.

Q: Is it okay that my dream doesn't involve saving the polar bears or curing breast cancer? All I want is to make a ton of money and never work again.

A: Financial freedom is a glorious goal. It was on my list of things to figure out. I'm grateful I did. That said, a truly rich life comes from what we contribute. The folks I know who have generated real (not inherited) wealth center their lives on contributing to others. Not one wealthy, respected person I know spends their time sipping margaritas on the beach or making it rain at the club. They're motivated, active, and constantly challenging themselves to learn more, do more, give more, and be more. They each generate and share tremendous goodness with the world through their jobs, businesses, friendships, creative expressions, and philanthropic endeavors. So by all means, get that coin. Just know that you'll be superrich—in every sense of the word—when you make life about what you can give, not what you can get.

One final note in this vein. Never, ever forget that everyone struggles. I mean everyone. My career has afforded me a front row seat to some of the most creative, accomplished people on the planet. Regardless of wealth, fame, or perceived power, every single individual is fighting their own private battles. We all have our vulnerabilities and insecurities. Money is wonderful. But it doesn't solve all problems. Humans need meaningful projects to work on. We need strong, loving relationships. We need a reason to get up in the morning. We need to connect and contribute. Otherwise, we get destructive. Don't believe me? Read up on the nightmare lives and suicides of lottery winners. Then check out how many retirees die soon after they stop working, or get so bored and depressed that they reenter the workforce.

Q: What if my dream isn't big, epic, or long-term? Is it all right if it's fairly small?

A: Size is subjective. An epic dream for one person might be child's play for someone else. We all have different skills and appetites for achievement in life. Despite popular opinion, big dreams aren't necessarily better dreams.

First, big dreams can be paralyzing and counterproductive, particularly when our confidence has taken a hit. Or when we're crushed under the weight of extraordinary physical, psychological, or emotional pain. The wins from microdreams like getting out of bed, going for a daily walk, or even calling a friend can make the difference between life and death. There's nothing small about that.

We humans thrive off of progress. We're motivated by momentum. I always chunk larger goals down into more immediately achievable projects. Right now, I'm focused on finishing just this chapter, not the entire book. So stack up those small wins. That's how all big things get done. Starting small doesn't mean thinking small.

This next point is rarely, if ever, considered. Artificially forcing yourself to commit to a big long-term goal can be counterproductive. Perhaps what you're destined to do or become in the next three, five, or ten years doesn't even exist yet! (See chapter 8: Progress Not Perfection, for more on my experience with this.) So attempting to envision a huge goal and then locking yourself into that path *might* be the worst thing you could do. Trying will only produce tears and frustration, making you feel like a visionless loser. Instead of shoehorning yourself into a long-term dream, shift your lens. Think short-term. Get hyperfocused on an important, modest dream that's immediately in front of you. Whether that's mastering a new technique in Photoshop, cleaning the garage, securing a second part-time job, getting back to the gym, writing your first short story, or anything else—achieving what's pressing in your life right now will help you develop focus, discipline, and confidence. More often than not, conquering small, immediate goals builds momentum and confidence for big tasks down the road.

Finally, don't underestimate the power of honoring your unique dreams. You were encoded with irreplaceable genius, born from unrepeatable chemistry, which includes the size and scope of your dreams. There is no one-size-fits-all. Your journey is unlike anyone else's. If signing up for a bird-watching class at your community college is the dream that lights you up, DO IT. Whatever sets your heart on fire and makes you come alive, that's what you should focus on. Right now, your soul is *screaming* to be heard. Its role is to guide the unfolding of your life. Listen to it. Follow your quirky inclinations, no matter how obscure or insignificant they seem.

Q: What if my dream is so big it's paralyzing? What if I freeze up when I think about the scale?

A: If solving world hunger or ending gender inequality is among your dreams, I commend you. You're one of the primary reasons I wrote this book. We need the full activation and diversity of skills, talents, and perspectives to make these big changes happen. At first blush, monumental dreams seem impossibly out of reach. But if we start where we are and with what we have, they're actually more possible than you'd think. That's how all great historic transformation has ever come about. We must also accept that sweeping cultural change happens in stages. We may not cross the ultimate finish line in our lifetime, but that doesn't mean we won't make tremendous progress and positively impact countless lives along the way. For example, pioneering feminist thinker Mary Wollstonecraft wrote *A Vindication of the Rights of Woman* in 1792. Yet it wasn't until 1920, a whopping 128 years later, when some US women won the right to vote. And it wasn't until 1965 when the Voting Rights Act fully protected Black Americans.

Fast-forward to 1970. Take a look at some of the US laws still on the books:

- Employers in most states could legally fire a woman for being pregnant.
- Banks could require a woman applying for credit to have her husband cosign.
- In twelve states, husbands could not be prosecuted for raping their wives.

Mind-boggling, right? At the time of this writing we're well into the twenty-first century and we're still fighting for equal pay. That doesn't mean Mary's work wasn't effective. Even though Mary didn't "figure out" gender equality in her lifetime, her work was a vital and important piece of the puzzle. She helped pave the way for the generations of women who came after.

Regarding some of our most painful collective problems, figuring out solutions is about the long game. If a moonshot goal is in your heart, start where you are. As Martin Luther King Jr. taught us, take the first step in faith. You don't have to see the whole staircase, just take the first step.

You don't have to save the world tomorrow. Start by making a difference to just one person today. Then make a difference to another. Then another. Everything in this book is applicable to you. Stop waiting. Start now.

Q: What if nothing seems that inspiring, exciting, or important? What if I just don't know what I want?

A: If you're dream anemic (and some people are), the following exercise will help you figure out what you really want. Plus, you'll understand why you haven't been getting it. It's intense and eye-opening. It requires seven days of written work, approximately ten to fifteen minutes per day. I highly recommend completing this written exercise by hand.

Begin writing, "What I really want is . . . ," and then keep writing until you fill the page. As many times as you need to, reuse the prompt "What I really want is . . ." and keep writing. Don't edit or censor yourself. Don't worry about spelling or grammar. Once you've filled the page, you're done for the day. Don't reread it yet.

Repeat this on a fresh sheet of paper for the next six days. On the seventh day, read all of the pages you've written and circle what's most repeated. Next, on a fresh sheet of paper, write "EVERYTHING IS FIGUREOUTABLE" at the top. Then, underneath, take the most repeated item and finish the following prompts:

I really want _____ [fill in the blank with your most repeated item] *because* . . . [fill in why this is important to you]

When I figure this out, I'll feel . . . [describe the emotions you'll feel]

The reason I believe I haven't been able to figure this out before is . . .

Truthfully, what I haven't been willing to do in order to figure this out is . . .

Now what I'm willing to do to figure this out is . . .

Once you're done, finish up the page by writing this line:

See, [insert your first name], *everything is figureoutable.*

Complete this exercise with an honest, open heart. You will not only know what you really want but also how to start figuring it out.

Whew! You did it.

If you've completed the exercises with your full effort (or are in the process of doing it), well done! You're on your way to mastering the figureoutable philosophy. But if you just thought about your answers or half-assed any of this, STOP.

Go back.

Do the work.

Grab a damn piece of paper and start writing, now.

(Plus, you'll need that one clear dream for what's coming next: a simple but effective strategy to fast-track your results.)

Figureoutable Field Notes

Instead of settling for the status quo, this couple figured out how to split their time between London and New Zealand.

We are Paul and Kim, a husband and wife from New Zealand who live in London—literally the other side of the world from home! After seven years in our new home and LOVING life, we became more conscious of being so far away from family—especially aging and unwell parents, friends, siblings, nieces, nephews, and godchildren.

We thought we had only two choices:

1. Give up our life, careers, apartment, and community in London, and move back to New Zealand permanently. (Nooooo!)
2. Use all our holiday allowance and savings to go back to New Zealand each year to visit. (But what's the point of living in London if you can't use some of your holidays to travel Europe?! And does once per year really cut it when you need real, quality time with your family?)

The challenge: How could we create a life (and job!) with location freedom so that we could spend more time in New Zealand, without sacrificing everything we'd built in London?

We experimented with option two and used all our holiday

allowance and savings to spend a month visiting home. It was stressful and a little soul destroying. On a car journey between cities, we had a long, deep, emotional chat about our life. We didn't want to move back to NZ permanently, but living and working in London wasn't sustainable either.

That's when we had a brainwave! What if we started our own business?! We could combine our skills, work from anywhere, and spend more time together as a result!

We were in the car, driving up the southern motorway in Auckland, when I signed up for B-School on my phone! We experimented with two businesses, one for each of us, before we realized that selling products *we* loved wasn't enough to make a successful business. *Other* people have to love them, too.

Our quote of the year was "Everything is figureoutable." Whenever we felt lost or defeated, it's what we would say to each other to pick ourselves up and keep going. Eventually, we worked out that two separate projects were dividing our energy. We needed to combine forces.

But it's one thing to be married for seventeen years and another to work successfully as colleagues. So we did the thing we'd been avoiding—proper market research. In doing that, we realized that actually, we were quite good at it. It perfectly combined our skills.

So, voilà, our business: helping entrepreneurs uncover customer insights. A year later, we have a small business with location freedom. We're writing this from sunny New Zealand, where we're spending three months with family and friends while working remotely with clients in four countries.

It's a dream come true! Not only can we spend quality time with our family without abandoning our life in London, but we've

(continued)

been able to realize other dreams, too—ones we had in our minds, but didn't have a way to make real . . .

1. Bonus Dream #1: We'll travel back to the UK via one month in California. We've always been fascinated by California—the sun, the beaches, Silicon Valley, and the yoga and green juice culture. Now we get to check it out!
2. Bonus Dream #2: When we first moved to London, one of our dreams was to live in a European country and learn another language, but we had no idea how to do that. But now it's real and happening! After California we'll be in Spain for two months living, working, and learning Spanish! Olé!

Everything is figureoutable has turned our lives upside down in the best possible way. We hope more people hear this phrase and are encouraged to go for their biggest dreams—even the ones they've given up on, like we had!

—PAUL AND KIM
LOCATION-FREE!

7

Start Before You're Ready

> "Are you ready?" Klaus asked finally.
> "No," Sunny answered.
> "Me neither," Violet said, "but if we wait until we're ready we'll be waiting for the rest of our lives."
>
> *Lemony Snicket*, The Ersatz Elevator

I was standing outside, looking up at the Viacom building in Times Square. Tourists and fast-moving business folks bumped me from all sides. My palms were sweaty. I was light-headed. Nauseated. I eyed the metal garbage can on the corner of Broadway and Forty-Fifth. *Should I throw up now or wait until I'm inside?* I felt like a complete fraud. Not one part of me felt ready for what I was about to do.

Let me explain.

Remember how I sobbed in my first real dance class at Broadway Dance Center? How I couldn't believe I'd wasted so many years thinking about dance rather than actually dancing? You should know, I barely made it through that class. Yet even though I had trouble following the choreography and didn't vibe with the music or dance style, that single class changed my life. It released my inner dance kraken. Mind you, I was still living on a blow-up air mattress in my friend's apartment, mired in debt and scraping by. Taking consistent classes at Broadway Dance Center didn't seem possible at the time (twenty dollars per class adds up fast), but I had to find a way to keep going. Thankfully, I had a membership to Crunch Fitness. Crunch was known for its innovative group fitness classes and had a strong roster of dance teachers.

Hip-hop was (and still is) my one true love; it's what I grew up listening to and still what makes me come alive. Aside from coaching and bartending, I started going to every hip-hop dance fitness class I could find on the schedule. I went uptown, downtown, and crosstown. I'd never learned choreography before and dove headfirst into the challenge. Although I was slow to pick up the combinations, I stuck with it. What I lacked in technique and experience I made up for in effort. This went on for several months until I was a bona fide Crunch class addict. I became a member of what we affectionately called the "front row mafia"—those people who show up early to class, claim their spot at the front of the room, and go full out. We're talking hair whips and stank faces. One day, something unexpected happened. After class, while I was still dripping with sweat and trying to catch my breath, the teacher came over to me and said, "You're a good dancer. You got energy. Have you ever considered teaching?"

I legitimately looked over each shoulder in disbelief. "WHAT?!?! ME?!?! TEACH?!?!?" My mind scrambled. I wondered, *Is she high? I have no clue what I'm doing.*

She continued, "We have teacher auditions coming up. You should try out."

Though I was stunned and skeptical, I was also intrigued. My self-esteem had been in the toilet for so long that it was encouraging to hear someone say that I was mildly good at something.

FUTURE TRIPPING DONE RIGHT: THE TEN-YEAR TEST

> There are two types of pain you will go through in life: the pain of discipline and the pain of regret. Discipline weighs ounces, while regret weighs tons.
>
> *Jim Rohn*

Back at home, I sat on my air mattress stressing over whether to give this teacher audition a shot. I was torn. No doubt, I loved what I was learning and felt so alive in class. But was it responsible to put time and energy toward this new thing when I desperately needed to grow my coaching business, make more money, and—I don't know—find a stable place to live? This was my fourth year of back-to-back career failures. I was estranged from my family and definitely wearing out my welcome at my friend's place. I felt an incredible pressure to get my shit together and be an adult. I was gripped with fear that pursuing dance would put me even further behind. Maybe even jeopardize my future. That's when I thought to ask myself a simple, illuminating question:

In ten years, will I regret NOT doing this?

In other words, when I'm thirty-five, will I look back at my twenty-five-year-old self and regret that I didn't take this chance to pursue dance and fitness more seriously?

ANSWER:

Abso-friggin-lutely.

I knew instantly (and viscerally) that thirty-five-year-old Marie would most certainly slap current-day Marie. *Hard.*

If you're unfamiliar with the term, "future tripping" refers to the common human tendency to worry about the future at the expense of living fully in the present. But when future tripping is strategic (like with the Ten-Year Test), stressing over future pain can be a powerful catalyst for change. Once I realized that thirty-five-year-old Marie would regret not at least exploring teaching dance, it was game time. I shifted my focus into figuring out how to best prepare for that audition. I asked for advice from as many dance teachers as I could. I worked my tail off to come up with a simple routine. Found bumping music. Practiced my cueing over and over and over again.

Audition day came. I was overly smiley and visibly nervous. But somehow I made it through my routine. I was given a long list of things to improve, but was now officially on the roster as a substitute teacher. Next, I started shadowing my favorite instructors—both in dance and general fitness classes. I always brought along a little yellow legal pad. Whenever I noticed a teacher say or do something inspiring, I'd crouch down, scribble a note, and then stand up and keep moving. My goal was to absorb everything I could about how to lead a great class. The more immersed I became in the world of dance and fitness, the more comfortable I began to feel in my own skin. This small but meaningful progress started impacting my coaching work, too. I began to communicate more clearly and succinctly. My energy and enthusiasm increased. Then one day, seemingly out of nowhere, I received a precious little mental download from the Career Gods. Their gift was a simple two-word phrase. But before I share it, some context . . .

INSPIRATION FROM THE ISLAND OF MISFIT TOYS

Normal is not something to aspire to, it's something to get away from.

Jodie Foster

I adore animated stop-motion Christmas specials. One of my favorites is the 1964 classic, *Rudolph the Red-Nosed Reindeer.* If you're not familiar with the story, Rudolph is ostracized from his reindeer community because he doesn't fit in. His big, red, glowing nose makes him a superfreak. Hurt and humiliated, he runs off into the woods where he encounters Hermey the elf, another young runaway. Consumed with shame, Hermey fled Santa's Workshop because he had zero interest in a toy-making career. Hermey had other aspirations—aspirations so unusual that when he shared them, he was laughed out of the North Pole. His ultimate dream: to be a dentist. Rudolph and Hermey decide to be misfits together and eventually wind up on the Island of Misfit Toys, the place where all the world's unloved or unwanted toys live. There, we meet a charming train with square wheels. A cowboy that rides an ostrich. And, my favorite, a jack-in-the-box who cries because he's named Charlie. "What child ever asks for a CHARLIE-in-the-box?!"

I consider myself an honorary resident of the Island of Misfit Toys. Like Rudolph and Hermey, I've always felt like I don't quite fit in. My choices regularly seem to go against the grain. That's why what I'm about to share—my surprise gift from the Career Gods—was so helpful. When I heard this two-word phrase for the first time in my head, it was as if someone else whispered it to me. It was like a secret clue was being revealed to nudge me along my misfit path.

Multipassionate
Entrepreneur
Marie . . .
You ARE a Multipassionate Entrepreneur.
Now quit whining about how I never give you signs.

This little made-up phrase was transformative at that stage in my life. From that moment forward, and without much forethought, when people asked me what I did for a living, I started saying that I was a multipassionate entrepreneur. Rather than feeling shame because I didn't have one good, society-approved answer, I began to feel just the slightest twinge of swagger. Whenever I said "multipassionate entrepreneur," people were intrigued and asked what that meant. I'd then share a bit about all the things I did for a living: my coaching practice, working as a personal assistant for a photographer, bartending, *and* that I was starting work in dance and fitness. That phrase gave me a new context, and in doing so, I began to see myself in a new light. Which, unsurprisingly, led to new opportunities.

Our culture is steeped in outdated understandings of careers, callings, and livelihood. A significant portion are relics of the industrial age and the push for specialization. Long before you're a functioning adult, you're expected to choose one (well-paying) thing to be, incur outlandish debt to get educated in that one thing, stick to that choice for the next forty-plus years, pray you'll earn enough to one day retire, and not go broke before you die. Not only is this idea grossly passé but it's dangerous in myriad ways—one being that many of us simply aren't built for that kind of narrow, long-term focus.

Sure, some people instinctively and happily devote their lives toward a single field. They're clear and enthusiastic, sometimes even as children. I *must* become a _____. Writer. Builder. Musician.

Neuroscientist. Sales executive. Mathematician. Engineer. Inventor. Lawyer. Actor. Etc. We love those folks. You may be one of them.

But some of us aren't designed that way. We're multipassionate creatives. We connect the dots between diverse and often seemingly disparate disciplines, spanning years and even decades. Eventually (and usually in retrospect), we weave innumerable skills, experiences, and ideas into a multilayered, multifaceted, one-of-a-kind career tapestry.

One thing is certain: there is no set blueprint for discovering your life's work. We're each on a wholly individualized adventure. You must have the wisdom to keep faith with the signals from your heart and the courage to walk your own path.

Those two simple words—"multipassionate entrepreneur"—helped me finally stop trying to fit myself into a conventional career box and gave me the emotional freedom I needed to spread my misfit wings and fly.

THE NASTY LITTLE LIE THAT HOLDS YOU BACK

> A surplus of effort could overcome a deficit of confidence.
>
> *Sonia Sotomayor*

Cut back to me on the cusp of hurling into a public trash can outside the Viacom building. Just two weeks prior, I began teaching my very own hip-hop classes at a Crunch gym. As luck would have it, a producer from MTV was a student in one of those early classes. After the cooldown, she approached me and introduced herself. "Hey—I loved your music choices and energy! You know, I'm working on a show and we've got an opening for a choreographer/producer. You should come and meet my boss. I think you'd be *great* for this position."

Remember, I was still as green as you could get in the dance world. After all, I just started to teach my own class—and at a gym for heaven's sake, not a professional dance studio. Only a few short months had passed since that Beginner Modern Jazz cry-fest at Broadway Dance Center. Now I was faced with an offer to interview for a position at MTV. The thoughts in my mind sounded like this:

Oh HEEELLLL no! I'm SO not ready for this yet!! C'mon, Universe. Couldn't this opportunity show up just a little bit later—once I figure out what the hell I'm actually doing? When I'm more experienced? More confident? More, you know . . . R E A D Y?

But here's the truth I've come to learn time and time again:

You never feel ready to do the important things you're meant to do.

As panicked as I felt, I couldn't justify a flat-out no. I grew up watching MTV! They were an epic brand. Plus, I needed to make more money. I had to at least give it a shot. So I'd said yes, scheduled an interview, and showed up as a queasy, clammy mess outside the Viacom building. After a few deep breaths, I walked in, cleared security, and stepped into the elevator. On the ride up to the twenty-fourth floor, I got my head straight. I committed to give it my all. This was a once-in-a-lifetime opportunity. I wasn't getting any younger, and I knew I'd regret it if I let fear hold me back.

Plus, this experience could help me gain something else I desperately wanted: a way to exponentially speed up my learning. Immersion in the MTV environment would force me to grow as a dancer, choreographer, and leader at ten to twenty times the speed than if I was stumbling around, trying to piece things together by myself. I arrived on the twenty-fourth floor and walked down the hall to the boss's office. I shook out my hands, shimmied my shoulders, rolled my neck, then knocked on her door. Long story short . . .

I booked that gig.

Honestly, getting the job was even more terrifying because I suddenly had to lead, manage, and creatively support dancers that had years more experience than I did. My naivete was, at times, glaringly obvious. There were dance terms thrown around in conversation I didn't know, never mind perform. I felt like a clueless idiot on a regular basis.

And yet that one decision to say yes, far before I was "ready," was a launching point for what became a string of incredible projects that parlayed into an extremely satisfying segment of my career. Because of this one choice, I would later star in and lead a number of dance fitness videos, choreograph commercials, become a Nike athlete, and travel the world.

It's not an exaggeration to say that that single decision to start *before* I was ready profoundly impacted the entire course of my business and life. The connections I made, the skills I strengthened on camera (hello, future *MarieTV!*), and the production experience I gained from one single move were enormous. I also maintained my coaching clients and a number of bartending shifts, too, which meant that I learned how to manage my time like a boss. What's more, I continue to use this **start before you're ready** strategy to fast-track my learning and growth.

These days, I run toward projects that make me uncomfortable, and not once has starting before I felt ready failed to produce valuable results.

On *MarieTV* I interview some of the world's most creative and accomplished people, and guess what—virtually all of them share stories of starting before they felt ready. I bet you have proof of this in your own life, too. Haven't some of your most valuable growth experiences come because somehow you bypassed the pervasive little *"I'm not ready yet"* lie? Because you moved ahead despite fear, hesitation, and uncertainty? My hunch is yes. That's because of this timeless truth:

All progress begins with a brave decision.

Personal progress. Professional progress. Collective, societal progress—all of it is born from a single person's decision to act. To stand up. To speak out. To make a move. Usually long before there's any guarantee of success. Another point most of us fail to see: action comes *before* the courage to act. **Action spawns courage, not the other way around.**

Action also generates motivation. Instead of waiting for inspiration to strike, action implores you to keep going.

Think about working out. You don't always feel like doing it. In fact, you might very strongly *not* want to do it. Listen to the voice in your head and you'll hear something like, *I don't FEEL like it. I'm tired. I don't want to. I'll start tomorrow.* However, something peculiar happens the moment you lace up your sneakers and get moving anyway. Another, more powerful force takes over. Within a few minutes, you feel more energized and alive. Inspired, even. Work out a few days in a row and BAM—a domino effect kicks in. Without much effort, you begin to crave healthier foods. Drink more water. Maybe even yearn for your next workout. This same phenomenon can be seen with virtually any creative endeavor. Bodies in motion tend to stay in motion. Doing it generates the desire to keep doing it.

That's why this "start before you're ready" practice is a vital part of the figureoutable philosophy. When you start before you're ready, you obliterate inertia and get momentum on your side. This applies to anything we want to figure out. Momentum is the secret elixir, and the only way to get that momentum is this:

You must disobey the voice in your head
that says, *I'm not ready yet*.

Know why? Because that voice is bullshit. It's a lazy, whiny, repetitive, life-sucking little parasite. That voice—the one that's constantly telling you how *not* ready you are, how much you don't feel like doing this or that, how incapable and incompetent and not good enough you are—that voice is not you and it's not true. The only power it has is the attention and authority you grant it. Stay aware, because the voice is cunning. It'll do whatever it can to keep you caged in stuckness with logical, rational lies.

The timing isn't right.
I need to wait until _____ happens.
I'll make too many mistakes if I start now.
I don't have the knowledge.
I don't have my plan all mapped out yet.
I can't risk _____ until I know _____ will work out.

That voice is a one-trick pony. It wants to tell the same old tired story of how incapable you are. Don't be seduced. The faster you train yourself to disobey that voice, the faster you'll fortify your ability to figure anything out.

THE FINE PRINT ON HOW TO START BEFORE YOU'RE READY

The "start before you're ready" strategy means exactly what it says. Stop thinking and start doing. Make a move. Any move. Send the email. Register for the class. Pick up the phone. Schedule the meeting. Have the conversation.

This is why I was such a stickler that you make your dream actionable, measurable, and specific in chapter 6. A dream to "travel more" isn't nearly as easy to start as "go to surf camp in Costa Rica this summer." When your dream is chunked down, your next steps become painfully obvious. The following points will help you master the art of starting before you're ready.

1. BEWARE OF PROCRASTINATION DISGUISED AS "RESEARCH AND PLANNING"

Starting before you're ready doesn't mean you should be ignorant or haphazard. Depending on the nature of your dream and how much you already know, some initial research and planning may be necessary. For instance, to reach your ultimate dream of speaking conversational Spanish within the next twelve months, you might look into language immersion courses, research private instruction, and download a language app. That's fine.

But be warned: extensive research and planning is often a way to keep procrastinating. You can spend weeks, months, even years "preparing" without making any real, tangible progress. Research, especially online, can be particularly dicey. I've gotten myself sucked into multi-hour, multi-day research rabbit holes far too many times to count.

Remember, you don't need to know everything about your dream, nor do you need to map out every step in advance. Stop hiding behind books and websites. Instead develop a bias for action. Make appointments. Have real-life conversations. You'll learn more and make faster progress. Start before you're ready. Start before you're ready. Start. Before. You're. Ready.

If you must research, stay on task. The internet is a minefield of distractions that can gobble up the most precious resources you have: time and energy. Your objective should always be to get enough information to take your next active step, and nothing more. Don't rely on willpower either. The lures of hot links, ads, notifications, and emails are far too great. Instead, give yourself a clear research objective (the ONE thing you're looking to learn/find out/confirm/act on) and a set window of time to find it. Then set a timer, get the information you need, and take action on it immediately.

2. GET SKIN IN THE GAME

Find a way to put your time, money, and/or ego on the line. Create games that have real-world, painful consequences if you don't keep moving. Cognitive psychology and decision theory show that we humans have something called loss aversion. That means we much prefer avoiding losses to acquiring gains. Let's say a twenty-dollar bill accidentally falls out of your pocket and you lose it. That loss will hurt significantly more than the happiness you'd feel if you found twenty dollars on the ground.

One way to get skin in the game is to make a financial commitment. Early in my career I was terrified of speaking in public. I knew it was an important skill, so I joined a local Toastmasters group. The membership fee was around fifty bucks. I was barely scraping by, so on top of genuinely wanting to improve my public speaking, I really didn't want to waste that cash. As I got more involved in the group, I became friendly with the other members. Developing those social connections gave me another layer of "skin in the game." Not showing up to meetings meant I'd feel guilt, shame, and embarrassment—so I used that to further motivate myself to keep going.

There are unlimited digital tools to help you put skin in the game. Search online for *accountability apps + [the current year]*. You'll discover a treasure trove of options with a wide array of features. The basic format is this: You set your goal (e.g., write five hundred words a day, five days a week) and determine the financial fine you'll pay if you don't stay on track. If you fail to take action, you lose that money. Some apps even allow you to determine what happens to the money you lose. You can have that cash sent to your nemesis or to an anti-charity—a cause or an organization you can't stand. That's taking loss aversion to the next level.

No matter what method you use, putting skin in the game helps you power past procrastination. Don't dick around. Your life is at stake. Do whatever it takes to start—now.

3. VALUE GROWTH AND LEARNING OVER COMFORT AND CERTAINTY

Like many bootstrapping entrepreneurs, for those first few years of my business I did everything myself. I wore all the hats—marketing and delivering my service, scheduling, invoicing, website updates, content creation, email correspondence, customer service—you name it.

Eventually, I reached a breaking point. It was impossible to keep up with all the demands on my time. I knew I needed to hire help, but was terrified to make that move. I had very little revenue, so hiring someone seemed out of reach. I'd also never been a boss before. I had no clue how to find, hire, train, delegate, or manage another person.

It was all so overwhelming and unknown, but I had a critical choice to make. Either stay in my comfort zone and keep trying to do more, swim faster, pedal harder. Or I could grow and learn how to hire someone. I could start before I was ready and figure this out.

Instinctively, I knew if I stayed in my comfort zone much longer, I'd kill the very thing I was working so hard to build—my own business. My next move was clear. It was time to start living in what I now call the growth zone. Otherwise, there was no chance I'd ever move beyond the level I was at.

The growth zone is a magical, albeit scary-ass place. But it was the only place I could learn how to be a boss, how to delegate, and how to grow my business beyond myself. Entering the growth zone meant things would be uncertain. I'd feel uncomfortable. I would also likely fall flat on my face. A lot.

Guess what? I did. I made tons of mistakes. At first, I hired the wrong people. I was horrible at delegating. There was enormous self-doubt, insecurity, and tears. But once I planted my feet firmly in that growth zone, I refused to give up. There was no turning back. Eventually, I started to get it right.

In the comfort zone, which is where most of us spend way too much time, life feels safe. Even if things are stressful, at least you feel secure in the fact that it's familiar. You're accustomed to the patterns, no matter how dysfunctional. It's the beast you know.

But everything you dream of becoming, achieving, or figuring out exists in the growth zone (aka the *discomfort* zone). When you're in the growth zone, here's what's guaranteed: you will feel vulnerable and insecure, but in order to grow, you must let go (at least temporarily) of your need for comfort and security. You must train yourself to value growth and learning above all else.

The growth zone is where you'll gain new skills and capabilities. It's where you acquire strength and expertise, and produce new results. Hang in the growth zone long enough and something marvelous happens. That growth zone becomes your *new* comfort zone.

All the things that once felt so terrifying no longer faze you. Your confidence increases, which strengthens your conviction to tackle the next set of challenges. You begin to expect and embrace the uncertainty, vulnerability, and humility embedded in every learning experience. This cycle is fundamental to mastering the figureoutable philosophy.

Almost everything you need to make your dream a reality requires new skills, experiences, and understanding. You must do things you've never done before. Starting before you're ready isn't easy, but if you want change—it's required.

INSIGHT TO ACTION CHALLENGE

Do the thing and you will have the power.
Ralph Waldo Emerson

1. *Recall at least one instance in your life when—either by choice or circumstances beyond your control* (e.g., job gain, job loss, a forced move, a birth or death, divorce, etc.)—you *started before you were ready* and ultimately gained valuable results.

2. *When was a time you delayed taking action because you believed you weren't "ready" yet, but once you did you thought,* Hey, that wasn't so bad. Why didn't I do this sooner?

3. *Answer fast:* As it relates to your big dream, what's the one move you know you must make to start before you're ready? What action step immediately enters your mind and heart? That *scary* big one you instinctively know will jump-start progress? Write it down and say it out loud.

4. *How can you commit time or money or use social accountability* (i.e., positive peer pressure or the fear of guilt, shame, or embarrassment) to take a big step forward on your dream? Put some skin in the game and make your move now!

Don't forget: The Ten-Year Test belongs in your Figureoutable Toolkit.

Do the Ten-Year Test (or Five-, Fifteen-, or Twenty-Year Test—the time frame should match what feels most appropriate to your situation) anytime you're faced with making a tough decision that could significantly impact the trajectory of your future and the ultimate achievement of your dream. Ask yourself, *Ten years from now, will I regret NOT doing this?*

Many people limit themselves to using their rational, logical minds to find their answer. Don't make that mistake. As first discussed in chapter 5 about fear versus intuition, notice what you feel. Your body contains wisdom and intelligence that's designed to help you figure things out.

Become aware of what happens viscerally and emotionally in response to this question.

Figureoutable Field Notes

At twenty-seven, she transformed her family business from sinking in tax trouble to tripling revenue . . . all while battling breast cancer.

A little over three years ago, I had just taken over my family's business. It was still pulling in revenue, but the previous family member who was running it was sinking it fast. I mean majorly—fraud, tax trouble, not paying vendors, and not responding to customers. He was six months behind on company bills, with no money in reserve and false accounting. I took over the business and had to quickly learn the ropes. (I come from the marketing and branding world and my family business is in manufacturing and engineering.)

Now I was using the *everything is figureoutable* method constantly. There were no records, everything was a mess, and I basically had to reinvent a very established company.

Then, four months later, I was diagnosed with breast cancer at age twenty-seven. That was definitely not in the plan! I now had to figure out how to run a business that supported my whole family, plus battle the beast that is breast cancer.

It was all figureoutable. I researched and implemented remote systems so I could work from my bed or the hospital. I learned to delegate and hire experts to help. I created an "ATTACK LIST" (a powerful to-do list) to accomplish everything I needed to.

Knowing that everything is figureoutable gave me a sigh of relief during a time I really needed it. It calmed down my team and family members to know that it would all work out. I pushed through and tripled my business revenue. Grew my team. Beat breast cancer.

—AMANDA
TEXAS

8

Progress Not Perfection

> Perfection is unachievable: It's a myth and a trap and a
> hamster wheel that will run you to death.
>
> *Elizabeth Gilbert*

Look. I'm a little freaky. I have high and somewhat idiosyncratic standards. My pasta sauce must simmer for no less than twelve hours. I karate chop my throw pillows for aesthetics (don't knock it till you try it). I like all of my cloth napkins folded in a particular, uniform way (Josh loves it when I correct him on this one). My creative director and I laugh at our shared "affliction"—we're typically the only two who notice the stray pixel on an otherwise impeccable design project. "Seriously, did no one else catch this glaring oversight?" So I understand the primal urge to keep polishing, tweaking, and refining to get something *juuuust* right.

Yet I've come to understand a crucial and sanity-saving distinction: having and holding yourself to high standards is not the same as perfectionism. Yes, they're related, but the former is healthy and motivating. The latter is dysfunctional at best and deadly at worst. Perfectionism at its core isn't about high standards. It's about fear. Fear of failure. Fear of looking stupid, fear of making a mistake, fear of being judged, criti-cized, and ridiculed. It's a fear that one simple fact might be true:

You're just not good enough.

Which, by the way, is unequivocally untrue. Sure, you may need to build skills and strengths to achieve your dream. Who doesn't? But the notion that you fundamentally don't have what it takes is a lie. That voice in your head that says so is just that same, repetitive, tired-ass shit-talker we discussed in the last chapter. The same voice we've now agreed to ardently disobey.

Know this: The fear of not being good enough is universal. Everyone—and I do mean everyone—wrestles with it. The problem occurs when this fear metastasizes into full-blown perfectionism. Be-cause perfectionism is paralyzing. Perfectionism keeps you suffering and spinning your wheels. But the dangers reach far beyond stuckness. Once perfectionism has a choke hold on your creative life force, it will stop at nothing to snuff you out.

THE PERILS OF PERFECTIONISM

Perfectionism is self-abuse of the highest order.
Anne Wilson Schaef

All too often we stop ourselves from doing anything new because we want so badly to get it right. (And get it right from the start, dammit.) We want to present an image to the world that we have it together. We have little to no tolerance for allowing ourselves the space and grace to be a beginner. Perfectionism isn't a set behavior, it's a destructive way of thinking about yourself. When you make a mistake (or, heaven forbid, fail), you don't just feel disappointment in how you did but in *who you are*.

Here's how destructive perfectionism can be. Between 2003 and 2006, researchers interviewed the friends and family of people who had recently killed themselves, and discovered something shocking. More than half of the deceased were described as "perfectionists" by their loved ones.[1] Another study revealed that perfectionists tend to die earlier while, by contrast, conscientious optimists tend to live longer.[2] In over twenty years of research, Dr. Paul Hewitt and his colleague Dr. Gordon Flett found that perfectionism correlates with depression, anxiety, eating disorders, and other mental health problems.[3]

Perfectionism is deadly. It's harmful to your health, happiness, and productivity. In a sad and ironic twist, it's often the primary blocking device that prevents you from becoming, achieving, and feeling your best. Nothing about it is helpful.

Now for some good news: dismantling perfectionism is 100 percent possible. Even better, you don't have to lower your standards to do it. In fact, without the toxic overlay of perfectionism, you're more likely to produce higher-quality work. You'll enjoy the process and give yourself room to experiment. And your one-of-a-kind potential that's been trapped inside? It'll explode onto the main stage of your life.

This isn't a negotiation. Pulverizing perfectionism, in all of its shape-shifting forms, is mandatory. It's as critical to mastering the figure-outable philosophy as oxygen is to your life. Let's begin.

MY CRINGEWORTHY WORKSHOP

When I first began my journey as a coach, I had a dream to one day work with large groups of people. I imagined myself speaking on a stage in front of thousands. I'd seen master speakers and teachers in action and wanted desperately to reach that level. It was an exciting vision, but my reality was much different.

I was at the embryonic stage of my business. I had barely any paying clients and made the majority of my money bartending. I lived in a four-hundred-square-foot studio and ate an alarming number of PB&J sandwiches.

Still, I was unbelievably passionate about the concepts and strategies I was learning in my training. Keeping all this newfound wisdom to myself felt criminal. *Why is this stuff not taught in school?!?! How come more people don't know that they can really change their life? This is so powerful!* I felt like Violet Beauregarde in *Willy Wonka & the Chocolate Factory*—if I didn't get this personal development juice out of me soon, I was going to burst like a swollen blueberry! So twenty-three-year-old me decided to spread the good word by holding my first-ever public workshop.

My friend Claire was kind enough to offer her basement as the venue. I named the workshop "How to Create a Life You Love." I created official workbooks using Microsoft Word, some very sophisticated clip art, my home printer, and a stapler. Finally, to make extra sure the crowd could follow along, I got myself a big easel, a flip chart, and some markers. *BOOM*. I was ready to rumble.

I'll have you know that my first public workshop was incredibly well attended . . .

By five people.

Claire, two neighbors that she literally dragged off the street, and my parents (God freakin' bless them). I cringe thinking about myself handing out those handmade, stapled workbooks to all five of my participants. I want to bury my head under the covers remembering the feeling of standing at that huge easel and making these adults—all at least twice my age—complete my workbook exercises. *So sad, so pathetic*, says the critical, mean-girl voice in my head.

In retrospect, there's nothing pathetic about it. I did something. I took a risk. I gathered those five people together. I gave my best effort. Not to mention, I likely had the worst event of my entire career behind me. *It's all uphill from here, baby!* That basement workshop gave birth to a simple directive I use anytime I sense perfectionistic tendencies perking up to stop me. Write this one down:

Starting small and sucky beats staying stucky.

Making it through that first workshop meant two important things. First, I beat the pants off my perfectionism. If I could do it once, I could do it again. Second, I was one step closer to my ultimate dream of one day teaching in front of thousands. Giving myself the space and grace to suck is the only way I've gotten remotely good at anything.

Every pro starts off as an amateur. There's not one top artist, athlete, writer, scientist, architect, entrepreneur, programmer, musician, or potter who enters the field at the top of her game. To begin anything new or learn anything new means you will be a neophyte. You must go from outsider to insider. Respect that. Embrace it. Be willing to suck.

Remember, perfectionism is a poisonous serpent. Its aim is to strike at your creative jugular. Here's one of its most cunning and lethal moves: getting you to compare yourself to accomplished masters.

I'm never going to be as good as _____,
so why bother trying?

Do NOT go there. Comparison is creative kryptonite. Remember, doing shots of Comparschläger can kill you.

No matter what form your creations take, chances are, it's not going to come pouring out of you all at once. Don't buy into the romantic idea that if you were really good at what you do—or really meant to do this—it would all flow effortlessly. For some rare people (cyborgs?), perhaps it does. But for most of us mortals, great work doesn't ooze out of our pores. We bleed and struggle and sweat for it. The process isn't neat or clean, and there's no secret formula.

The moment you measure your early efforts against someone who's been working their ass off for years—you've fallen into a perfectionist death trap. The fix for this is one magical mantra. Read this out loud:

Progress not perfection.

From this moment forward, that's all you strive for. Progress not perfection. Capisce?* That's the measuring stick you use to determine whether you're on track. That's all you care about. Did you make progress? Did you apply effort to learn and grow as it relates to what you want? It doesn't matter how small; progress is all you're after.

This is one of the core principles I drill into the hearts and minds of over fifty-four thousand B-School students. It's so transformative that at least one student had this mantra tattooed on her forearm. In tens of thousands of survey replies, "progress not perfection" is repeatedly cited as participants' most pivotal, game-changing breakthrough. It transforms your life by directing you to focus on the only things that matter—learning and growth. Plus, it prevents premature quitting and the mental agony that accompanies wondering if you should.

---

*Pronounced cah-PEESH. For my non-Jersey people: an Italian word mostly used by Americans to say "Got it?" or "Understand?"

Please understand, progress is never a straight line. Progress zigs and zags. It expands, then retreats. You will move forward and then back. Up and down. Then sideways and back again. To fight the erratic rhythm of progress is futile. Expect setbacks, stumbles, and big flops along the way. They're inevitable, and they're also positive indicators you're making progress.

PROGRESS MYTH:
What most people think progress looks like

Goal
Reached!

Starting Point

PROGRESS REALITY:
What progress actually looks like

Goal
Reached!

Starting Point

Don't be afraid of the ups and downs. Instead, prepare creative ways to deal with and learn from them. Expect that it will feel like you're making one step forward, then taking four back. Above all, cultivate patience. This is one of the most critical mental strengths of the figureoutable philosophy. Everything you want to create, achieve, or experience will likely take longer than you hope. Much longer.

Molly, one of our B-School students, illustrates this. When she first considered striking out on her own, she was working in a terrible job. She had no idea what she could do for a business or how she was going to pull it off, but she watched a video interview I did with another graduate and became deeply inspired. She wrote, "The woman you spoke with on video talked about having her first $30,000 month. When I heard that, I was like 'Holy shit, I WANT that. I will have that!'"

She came up with a business idea and worked on it for two straight years. But Molly couldn't get traction. She was heartbroken and felt like a failure. She couldn't afford to keep her business going and was on the verge of quitting, which is when she reached out to us via email. We gave her some coaching and suggested she also share her experience in our private community. Molly bravely posted about her struggle (a struggle that is so incredibly common, but when you're going through it, it makes you feel alone). She was flooded with support, ideas, and constructive feedback. She took a fresh look at her business and what she could improve. Emboldened, she refocused her efforts and energy. One year later, we received another email from Molly.

> I'm swinging by to tell you that so far this month I have made $31,255.00 (and it's only the 17th!!). It's surreal thinking back just three years ago. I still can't believe this is my life. It's such hard work, but it's worth every second.

Naturally, we were thrilled for her, but a few days later we got another note.

Can you let your team and Marie know that our final number for December was $65,300? Holy cow, we're still trying to process it!

Not only did Molly surpass the revenue goal that initially inspired her three years earlier, but she doubled it within a few weeks. Can you imagine if Molly had given up because she believed that two years of "failure" meant she wasn't making progress? Here's the truth: she was in fact moving forward, even though it didn't feel like it. Molly was wise enough to step back, evaluate her efforts, and ask for constructive feedback. She used that insight to adjust and keep going. To be clear, Molly's big win wasn't just about the money. It was about *who she had to become* in order to bring her once-impossible dream into reality. By focusing on progress not perfection, she became a person who figured things out. Now that capability will serve her for life.

I've heard countless variations of this story across every realm of business, art, filmmaking, writing, sports, relationships, health—you name it. Everything worthwhile takes time. More time than our impatient minds believe it should.

If you're clear that achieving your dream (or solving a specific problem) is still important, be patient. Stay on your grind. As Confucius supposedly said, it does not matter how slowly you go so long as you do not stop.

DON'T JUDGE YOUR
FLOPS TOO FAST

When I began taking my dance ambitions seriously, going to Broadway Dance Center (BDC) and Crunch, I developed certain ideas about what becoming a successful dancer meant. I overheard the pros talking about going on auditions and thought, *Oh, of course. That's what* real *dancers do. They go on auditions. Success = booking music videos, shows, and tours.* If I had any hope of becoming a real dancer, I figured I'd need to start auditioning, too.

Before long, I learned that Missy Elliott was looking for dancers for her new music video. I was out-of-my-mind excited. This was my chance! The audition was in Midtown Manhattan. When I popped up from the subway, a line of dancers snaked around the block. Everyone seemed to know one another, amiably chatting as they stretched and freestyled right on the sidewalk. I stood there frozen, with knots in my stomach.

After two hours of torture, I made it into the building and reached the third-floor walk-up. I handed over my headshot with my sparse ré-sumé stapled to the back and joined the next group of dancers in the open studio. The choreographer turned on the music and ran through a few moves. She was fast. I barely caught the first four counts while the other dancers seemed to instantly absorb the intricate choreography. Next thing I knew, the audition began and I had *no* idea what was going on. I couldn't keep up. To say that I was in over my head is an extraordinary understatement. My worst dance nightmare was coming true. After a few minutes, I was so embarrassed that I ran out of the studio in tears.

I walked down Eighth Avenue in a daze. *Who are you kidding thinking you could do this? You have no talent. You have no training. You're too old. Too slow. You'll NEVER make it!*

After a few days of licking my wounds, I forced myself to get back into class. I realized that the ability to pick up choreography quickly wasn't an inborn superpower; it was a skill, one I could (very) slowly improve. I kept training and kept going. But that Missy Elliott fail, as embarrassing as it was, was still progress. It inspired me to get honest about where I thrived in the dance world. What did I really enjoy? What was my endgame, and what would I have to do to get there?

Asking those questions—and really thinking about what success would look like in my real life, rather than in the abstract—was a game changer.

To be a "successful dancer," according to my narrow definition, I thought I needed to hustle to book tours with musical artists. Those gigs would mean living and working on the road. But at the time, I was also bartending, running my coaching practice, and was in the early stages of my relationship with Josh. What I believed *should* be the goals and aspirations of a conventional pro dancer weren't the right match for my multipassionate self.

I kept working on dance, but gave myself permission to focus my energy where I felt most alive. As much as I appreciated taking classes at BDC, dance fitness at Crunch was unbelievably fun. I made friends more easily because the work was rooted in joy and learning. I loved dancing alongside people of all different shapes, ages, and walks of life. It felt collaborative not competitive, and I was excited to put in the extra hours to grow.

Then something peculiar happened. When I stopped forcing myself to pursue conventional dancer goals, I started getting offers to appear in and create workout DVDs (remember those?) and partner with brands like *Shape* and *Prevention* magazines. As I gained more experience and made more connections, I booked gigs with big companies like VH1 and the Home Shopping Network. I taught at global conventions all while learning, growing, dancing, and having the time of my life. I let go of striving for conventional dancer goals and allowed myself to pursue my own unique path.

A few years later, an exciting opportunity appeared. Nike was launching a brand-new dance fitness initiative called the Nike Rockstar Workout. It was something that had never been done before by a global athletic company—introducing dancers as athletes. Jamie King, a dancer, choreographer, and creative director who's worked with the likes of Rihanna, Madonna, and Bruno Mars, was spearheading the initiative. Nike and Jamie brought the project to NYC and, long story short, I became one of the world's first Nike Elite Dance Athletes. I spent several years working and training with Nike around the globe, dancing on big stages, training hundreds of instructors, and doing the exact kind of work I loved.

Here's what's interesting: when I bombed that Missy Elliott audition years earlier, Nike Elite Dance Athletes didn't exist yet. There's no way I could have dreamed to reach that specific goal, because no one had done it before! It simply had not been created.

But my Missy failure spurred a necessary shift in my focus, pushing me to spend the next few years *unknowingly* training in the exact mix of hip-hop, dance, and fitness that prepared me to win that Nike position when it appeared!

Don't be so quick to judge your supposed failures. A flop might be a cosmic redirect, guiding you to a better, bigger purpose. Sometimes, as Missy would say, you must ask, "Is it worth it? Let me work it. Put your thing down, flip it, and reverse it."

CHARACTERISTICS OF PROGRESS VS. PERFECTION

If I waited for perfection, I would never write a word.
Margaret Atwood

There's a fine line between striving for excellence and getting sucked into a perfectionism sinkhole. The following will help you self-diagnose and self-correct.

THE THOUGHTS BEHIND PERFECTION VS. PROGRESS

Perfection	Progress
I have only one shot at this. If I fail/lose/get rejected, it means I suck and I should quit.	*I'll take as many shots as I can. I'll learn from every attempt. I'll get stronger and better.*
It's either ALL or NOTHING. If I can't get everything I want now, what's the point?	*I'll start small and simple now, then iterate and evolve over time.*
Failure is unacceptable. *I'm a failure. Always have been, always will be.* ***I always fail at everything. This will CRUSH me.*** *If I fail, I'm done. I can't go on.*	***Failure is inevitable.*** *My attempt may fail, but I'm not a failure.* ***Failure isn't permanent or personal.*** *Failure is an event, not a characteristic.*

Perfection	Progress
Ugh. Why is she so much more successful than me? I'm smarter, more genuine. OR, I'll never be that good.	She's so damn inspiring. I really connect with her vibe. If she can do it, so can I.
This has to happen immediately. ASAP! Give me a shortcut/hack/ formula. I need this to be easy. I can't handle challenges. I'll fail.	I'm in this for the long term. All great things take time. I'm ready to work hard. I'm excited for the challenge.
I feel discouraged and unsure. That means I'm a LOSER. Being uncertain and insecure is a sign that I'm out of my league and should quit.	**I feel discouraged and unsure.** That means I'm making PROGRESS! Being uncertain and insecure is a sign that I'm in new territory.
I can't handle another setback. I'm too weak. This is too hard.	Setbacks and obstacles? Bring it. Doing hard things makes me stronger.
Nothing is ever good enough. I can't show this to anyone until it's perfect.	Done is better than perfect. Real-world feedback helps me learn and improve.
FEAR ORIENTED: What will they think of me? What will everyone say about me?	CURIOSITY ORIENTED: What can I learn from this? How can I improve?

MIND THE GAP

In my tenure at Nike, I regularly traveled to Europe for training and events. While in London, I appreciated the constant reminders on the Underground to "mind the gap." Meaning, open your eyes and be aware. Don't face-plant when crossing the space between the train door and the station platform.

Similarly, we need to mind the gap on our figureoutable journey, particularly as it relates to choosing progress over perfection. There's a significant gap between what we *feel, see, and know in our hearts* about the change we want to make, and our capacity to pull it off. In other words . . .

Mind the gap between your ambition and your ability.

One of the best articulations of this creative gap comes from Ira Glass, the host and producer of the NPR show *This American Life* (bolding for emphasis is mine):

> [A] thing that nobody tells people who are beginners—and I really wish somebody had told this to me—is that all of us who do creative work . . . we get into it because we have good taste. But it's like there's a gap, that for the first couple years that you're making stuff, what you're making isn't so good, okay? It's not that great. It's really not that great. It's trying to be good, it has ambition to be good, but it's not quite that good. But your taste—the thing that got you into the game—**your taste is still killer**, and your taste is good enough that you can

tell that what you're making is kind of a disappointment to you, you know what I mean?

A lot of people never get past that phase. A lot of people at that point, they quit. And the thing I would just like to say to you with all my heart is that **most everybody I know who does interesting creative work, they went through a phase of years** where they had really good taste and they could tell what they were making wasn't as good as they wanted it to be—**they knew it fell short, it didn't have the special thing** that we wanted it to have.

And the thing I would say to you is **everybody goes through that**. And for you to go through it, if you're going through it right now, if you're just getting out of that phase—you gotta know **it's totally normal**.

And **the most important possible thing you can do is do a lot of work**—do a huge volume of work. Put yourself on a deadline so that every week, or every month, you know you're going to finish one story. Because it's only by actually going through a volume of work that you are actually going to catch up and close that gap. And the work you're making will be as good as your ambitions. It takes a while, it's gonna take you a while—**it's normal to take a while**. And **you just have to fight your way through that**, okay?[4]

There's an elegant typography video of Ira's spoken words that I highly recommend by filmmaker David Shiyang Liu. Search online for *Ira Glass + David Shiyang Liu video* to find it. Watch it daily until this truth seeps into every cell.

Figuring things out, creating real change, building skills, abilities, and understanding takes time and effort. Across all disciplines, concerning virtually all acts of creation—no matter who you are, what you want to do, achieve, experience, or solve . . .

Progress *not* perfection is the only way to bridge the gap between your ability and your ambition.

I've strived to mind the gap in every aspect of my life: from gaining physical strength at the gym, to renovating my home, to building a team, to developing my show *MarieTV*, which began on my old-school webcam with no editing, lighting, or film crew in sight.

So please, cooperate with the creative process, don't force it. Mind the gap.

Bit by bit, piece by piece, day by day. Focus on progress not perfection and you will successfully cross that chasm.

PROGRESS PUTS YOU IN A PRODUCTIVE MINDSET

You're in charge of your mind. You can help it grow by using it in the right way.

Carol Dweck

Carol Dweck, PhD, wrote one of my favorite books on this topic because it proves how the right mindset changes our behaviors and, most important, our results. In her book *Mindset,* Dweck, a Stanford University psychologist, discovered what she calls a "fixed mindset" versus a "growth mindset."

When you're in a fixed mindset, you believe that talent—without the application of *effort*—creates success. You're either born with it or you're not, and there's nothing you can do to change it. When in a fixed mindset, you'll avoid challenges, resist criticism, and perform for approval. This set of beliefs, and the behaviors that flow from it, are destructive.

In a growth mindset, you believe that your most basic abilities—like talent and intelligence—can be improved through effort, perseverance, and experience. In this mindset, whatever intelligence and abilities you're born with are just the start. People in a growth mindset crave challenges, welcome constructive criticism, view setbacks as *learning opportunities*, and develop a passion for hard work and a hunger for growth. They know that getting better is a process. One that requires the right attitude and dedication over time.

Here's the best part. At any given moment, you can choose your mindset. And the results of that choice can be life changing. Dr. Dweck tells the story of a struggling student named Jimmy, whom she described as one of the most "hard-core turned-off low-effort kids." After being taught about the fixed and growth mindset she writes that Jimmy "looked up with tears in his eyes and said, 'You mean I don't have to be dumb?'" From that moment on, Jimmy transformed. He stayed up late to do his homework and handed in assignments early, eager for feedback to improve. As Dweck wrote, "He now believed that working hard was not something that made you vulnerable, but something that made you smarter."[5]

Dweck highlights countless real-life examples of how these two different mindsets radically impact the results we create in our lives—

from parenting to education to sports. The evidence is undeniable. When you operate through a fixed mindset, you suffer. When you operate with a growth mindset, you develop a love of learning and resilience that leads to fulfillment and extraordinary accomplishment.

At this very moment, you can choose to put yourself in either a growth mindset or a fixed mindset. Just like you can choose progress instead of perfection. These are distinct choices with dramatically different outcomes. One leads to a life of pain and stagnation. The other to endless growth and fulfillment. Which will you choose?

SIX TACTICS TO PRACTICE

Use the following tactics to stay in the progress zone when the lure of perfectionism has pulled you off course.

1. TAKE SMALL STEPS AND IGNORE BIG DRAMA

Perfectionism loves drama. You'll start to notice that even before you've taken any steps toward fulfilling a dream, perfectionism will chime in with endless, berating questions. *Is my business idea even any good? How will I get it going? How am I going to manage dozens of people? What if I fail? What if I SUCCEED? I'll probably ruin my family. Everyone will be jealous of me. I'll lose friendships over this. Oh God, I'll wind up divorced and alone for the rest of my life . . .*

Don't indulge in this drama-fest. Keep your head down and do the work. Take small steps. Baby steps, even. Do them daily. Show up to the class. Build the prototype. Write your pages. Run your miles. Send the survey. Deposit one dollar. Be clean and sober for one hour. What-ever your dream is, get *obsessed* with making simple, daily progress. That's it.

You can scare yourself into stuckness by assuming you have to make radical life changes in order to make progress. You don't. **Real change is practically invisible as it's happening.** No trumpets sound. A marching band will not play at your door. Meaningful progress doesn't feel particularly exciting. Most days, it feels like work. You show up, grind it out (sometimes joyfully, sometimes not), and repeat.

So keep your eye on the prize: Take small steps daily and steer clear of big drama.

2. PLAN AHEAD FOR PROBLEMS

No matter how organized or motivated you are, things will knock you off track. From illness to technology fails to everyday interruptions, there will be loads of obstacles on your path. Anticipating and solving for them in advance is the key to steady progress. Here's how to do it.

First, think in microterms. What could derail your workday? Allow-ing text or email notifications? Taking unnecessary phone calls? Failing to stock the fridge? Then go bigger. What could take your whole project off track? Missed deadlines? Weather delays? Tech headaches? In our company, we noticed a pattern of delays related to design and develop-ment. We began to anticipate and solve for those problems in advance by regularly running through worst-case scenarios on any new project and brainstorming ways to handle them. It's not a foolproof system, but it helps. Ask yourself, "What potential problems could arise? What can I plan for in advance (even if it's my own emotional toughness) to miti-gate the negative impact of potential problems? What do I need to do now in order to keep making progress?"

3. EXPECT (AND EMBRACE) SELF-DOUBT

After the novelty of chasing your big dream has subsided, chances are you'll be swallowed by a tsunami of self-doubt. *WHY did I say yes to this?! This is all wrong. I can't do it. It's too hard. I don't have what it takes. Maybe I should just quit. Maybe I should change the whole thing and start from scratch. I hate this. I hate everything. I hate myself!*

Whether you're getting in shape, building a product, writing a screenplay, launching a new business or career, healing a relationship, or running for office—expect self-doubt to punch you in the gut.

I cannot emphasize how common this is. It usually happens more than once, especially on big projects. Everyone experiences this surge of self-doubt when moving beyond their comfort zone. This is a hallmark of progress, not a signal to stop.

As repeatedly mentioned (because people so often forget!), setbacks happen. They're not "signs from the Universe" that you should quit. (Obviously, if you discover you genuinely *don't* want to pursue this dream or goal anymore, then yes. Stop. Move on to something else.)

But if you're feeling disheartened, take a breath. Remember that self-doubt is normal. No matter how successful or experienced you become, self-doubt never fully goes away. Instead of saying, *What's the point?* ask yourself, *What's the next right move?*

4. ASK, "WHAT'S THE NEXT RIGHT MOVE?"

After a setback, ask yourself this question: "What's the next right move here?" Listen for the answer. It may be as simple as "drink a glass of water." Or "sleep on it." Or "you need some chips and hummus. Like, a lot of chips and hummus." Sometimes the next right move is taking a break to gain a fresh perspective. Go for a run. Work out. Dance.

Meditate. Take some space. Call a trusted, experienced, and supportive friend.

Or maybe when you ask yourself, "What's the next right move here?" you'll hear a response like, "That feedback stung, but there's truth in it. Use that insight to get even better." Or maybe you'll hear, "Stop judging yourself and *finish* this damn paragraph." Or perhaps, "Yes, we need to push our deadline back again. But we're not quitting. Let's refocus and keep going."

When you ask yourself, "What's the next right move?" you're directing your brain and heart to search for a productive answer.

5. USE THE POWER OF POSITIVE QUITTING

The old saying that quitters never win and winners never quit isn't true. Sticking with something *only* because you're afraid of looking like a loser is a terrible idea. There are times when you must be brave enough to cancel projects, goals, or relationships that no longer align with who you are or what you value.

Let me introduce you to the power of positive quitting. Positive quitting is when you realize that you've gone as far as you possibly can. You've given it your very best effort and now it's become clear—in your heart and soul—that the wisest and most productive next step is to cut your losses and move on.

In the early years of my coaching business, I invested months of time and significant money into building a private online membership community. This project was all-consuming and stretched me financially. When I finally launched, I was so excited. Hundreds of folks had registered and paid for access.

As soon as those new members started logging in, the entire thing crashed. I'm talking a totally frozen, tech-mess shitshow. Back then, I didn't have a support team. I was beyond embarrassed, but as upset as I was, I composed myself enough to step back, evaluate the situation, and take decisive action.

I pulled the plug. Naturally, I took care of my customers. I explained exactly what happened, transitioned them onto a stable, hosted platform, and delivered more than what I promised. But I wasn't about to sink more money, more time, and more energy into that custom site just to prove I could figure it out.

Sometimes, in the process of pursuing a project, you realize it's not actually what you want. It's clear: this is *not* what you want to keep doing. Even if your project doesn't crash and burn, you might choose to walk away because you're done. You've learned and experienced all you can and you're ready for the next chapter. Think about it like a buffet. You don't quit eating because something went horribly wrong. You stop eating when you're satisfied.

After about six years in dance and fitness, I wanted to devote 100 percent of my focus to my online business. So I walked away from my dance career. Not because there was anything wrong with it or because I failed, but because I was ready to evolve. Several years later, I decided to stop hosting an annual conference—one that generated over $1 million in revenue—not because there was anything wrong with the conference, but because I felt complete and wanted to work on other projects.

Whether it's a relationship, a career, or a project, just because something ends doesn't mean it failed. **Giving up isn't the same as moving on.** Don't use "progress not perfection" to punish yourself and keep pursuing a dream that no longer serves you. If, after a certain amount of time, you sense that it's time to pivot, do it. While there's no cut-and-dry formula to make these kinds of decisions, you've already learned two tools that help.

Tool #1. **The Ten-Year Test.** We first talked about this in chapter 7, and it's particularly useful here. Imagine yourself ten years into the future and ask, "If I end this right now . . . will I regret it then?"

　　When my expensive custom website crashed, I knew that in ten years' time I'd barely remember it. Yes, it was frustrating and I lost some cash, but it wasn't a soul goal. It was just one project that taught me many critical lessons.

Tool #2. Complete the **"What I Really Want"** seven-day writing challenge from chapter 6. It works miracles to help you gain clarity.

Also, revisit your Insight to Action Challenge work from chapter 6. Specifically, the second step: Get Real About This Dream. That's where you listed all of the reasons why pursuing this goal is important to you. Do a gut check. Are those reasons still valid and true? If yes, keep going. If not, you might be ready to move on. It takes courage to pursue a dream, but when that dream no longer fits, it can take even more to end it.

6. ABOVE ALL, CULTIVATE PATIENCE

"But, Marie, I've been working on my _____ [business, acting, writing, music, sculptures, recipes, screenplays, research, etc.] for at least _____ [three weeks, three months, or three years, etc.] and I'm going nowhere. What's wrong with me?! How long is this going to take?"

　　Answer: As long as it does.

Elizabeth Gilbert, author of the pop culture juggernaut *Eat, Pray, Love,* as well as seven other books so far, told me she didn't make a dime off her writing for the first ten years. Then, for the next ten years (which were *after* already having three books published), she still relied on various jobs outside writing to stay afloat. That's *twenty years* before she earned a living from her calling. During our *MarieTV* interview, Liz revealed a telling perspective on "doing whatever it takes" to support yourself as an artist. At fifteen, she made a sacred promise to her creativity. She said, "I will never ask you to provide for me financially, I will always provide for you." She promised to take whatever jobs necessary to fund the basics (food, rent, etc.) so that her creativity never had to carry the burden of keeping the lights on.

Steven Pressfield, author of a whopping seventeen titles, wrote for seventeen *years* before he earned his first penny as a writer—a $3,500 option on a screenplay that was never produced. He wrote for twenty-seven years before he got his first novel, *The Legend of Bagger Vance,* published. During all those years he worked twenty-one different jobs in eleven states.

As you know, I maintained a small constellation of side jobs for seven years before I was confident enough—emotionally or financially—to rely solely on my business for full-time income. Throughout those years, I seized every moneymaking opportunity I could to pay the bills. I cleaned toilets. Worked thousands of shifts as a bartender and waitress. My dream of running my own business, on my own terms, doing *exactly* the kind of work that I do now, was so important that I was willing to do whatever it took, for as long as it took, to see it through.

Cultivate patience. Don't believe the myth that if you were a "real" _____ [artist, performer, activist, scientist, entrepreneur, etc.] that you'd make a full-time living from your work. Perhaps it'll happen someday. But that's not always true, no matter how hard you work. There are countless creatives who are legitimate and admired who also supplement their income through a variety of unrelated means—teaching, seasonal work, service jobs, or rental income.

More importantly, there's no shame in doing whatever it takes to keep a roof over your head. Never be embarrassed about doing honest work. To say we live in a culture of instant gratification is a gross understatement. Don't get me wrong—I appreciate technology. But for some, it's all but destroyed the ability to cultivate patience. With a smartphone, you can watch almost any form of entertainment on demand. You can access a breathtaking and ever-growing collection of music, art, literature, and education, all at a moment's notice.

But the ease and speed of tech toys doesn't map to real life. To build skills, earn trust, develop a body of work, forge relationships, gain mastery, or solve complicated problems, it takes sustained, relentless effort. There are no shortcuts. If you're not willing to work your ass off over an extended period of time (I'm talking years, not months), then be honest with yourself: that dream isn't really that important to you. That's okay. Drop it. Dig deeper. Find something you are willing to stick with and work for, no matter how long it takes.

INSIGHT TO ACTION
CHALLENGE

Little by little becomes a lot.
Anonymous

1. *As it relates to your dream or problem, what's one thing you're stopping yourself from exploring because you're not willing to be anything less than perfect?* Or, if you prefer, use this prompt:

   If I didn't have to be perfect at it, I'd do/try/start _____ *to get closer to achieving my dream.*

2. *Who might you become and what might you accomplish if you focused on progress not perfection?* What might you learn? What strengths and skills could you develop?

3. *Plan (and solve for) problems in advance.* Brainstorm a list of typical challenges, distractions, and obstacles that could impede your ability to make progress. Think: social media sinkholes, internet outages, group texts, self-doubt spirals, missed deadlines, daytime calls from the family, and not having food in the house.

   For instance, if group text messages interrupt you all day, one solution is to put your phone on airplane mode or turn your phone completely off during focus time.

Whether the problem is internal or external, anticipate problems in writing and plan for solutions in advance.

4. ***Turn inevitable self-doubt into productive self-talk.*** Whenever you notice your inner monologue trash-talking you into a sinkhole of self-doubt, use this trick. Add the word "yet" to the end of thoughts that veer toward negative, dead-end, fixed-mindset thinking. For extra oomph, brainstorm a list of all the negative things you say to yourself that keep you from moving ahead. For example:

> I'm not good with money.
> I don't know the first thing about writing fiction.
> I don't know who I am without her.
> No one's ever done it this way.
> I don't know anything about running a business.
> I don't have any good ideas.

Say this instead:

> I'm not good with money *yet*.
> I don't know the first thing about writing fiction *yet*.
> I don't know who I am without her *yet*.
> No one's ever done it this way *yet*.
> I don't know anything about running a business *yet*.
> I don't have any good ideas *yet*.

You can say this in your head or write it down. Either way, this simple three-letter word "yet" will help you stay in the mindset of growth, learning, and progress.

5. *Grab a piece of paper and write this down:*

FIVE SMALL THINGS I CAN DO TODAY TO MOVE THIS PROJECT AHEAD

1.

2.

3.

4.

5.

Write at least five positive things you could do today to make progress. They don't have to be monumental. Just write whatever comes to mind. If you go past five, wonderful. Then underneath that list, write this:

ONE SMALL THING I CAN DO RIGHT NOW

_____

Choose one item from your list, write it down in big letters, and circle it (because circling it is fun). Say it out loud. Then DO IT! Bust yourself out of stuckville. Doing something is the secret to doing something.

Nice effort. Remember . . .

Life doesn't demand perfection. Life doesn't require you to be constantly fearless, confident, or self-assured. Life simply requires that you keep showing up.

Figureoutable Field Notes

Substance abuse, debt, suicidal thoughts, a nervous breakdown—everything is figureoutable helped Ula change her self-defeating habits, and become debt-free and healthy again.

I was a mess—emotionally, physically, mentally, and professionally. My beloved dad died of a brain tumor, I got married and divorced, I relocated to another country and needed to start all over again. I got into a passionate and toxic love affair that ended badly. Made a few wrong business decisions and ended up in great financial debt. All of this led to a massive breakdown. I was thirty-five.

I had nothing. No partner, no friends, no family, no job, no motivation to carry on. I felt like the biggest failure there is. I hated myself. I forced myself to get an easy job to pay my debt and monthly bills, but I hated the job and hated myself for doing it. I was a cleaning lady and believed I was unable to do anything else. I couldn't stand facing people. After hours cleaning apartments, I would come back to a little studio that desperately needed renovations. I hated it. I hated myself. I hated life. I was thinking about ways to end it. I drank liters of wine and smoked tons of cigarettes. Every evening the same. I drank, smoked, and cried myself to sleep.

One day, I heard about *MarieTV*. During my usual after-work routine of wine and cigarettes, I put on the episode "What to Do

When You Feel Useless and Alone." Marie was answering the question of a teenage girl. I cried tears of relief throughout the episode. I felt like I was that girl and that Marie was talking directly to me.

I didn't change my self-destructive habits immediately. I still hated myself and was ashamed of who I am, what I do, and where I got myself. Together with wine and cigarettes, though, I had *MarieTV*. Every evening I watched a few episodes. And with each day, with each episode, something was melting inside my heart.

One day, I woke up and decided to believe what she says, "Everything is figureoutable." I still didn't believe in myself, but I decided to believe Marie. She was the purest and most honest example of walking her talk. After work that day, I didn't buy wine and cigarettes. I put on my sneakers instead and went to the park for a run. It wasn't easy, but it felt like a major breakthrough.

Fast-forward to today and I'm back. I watch every episode of *MarieTV* (some repeatedly) and read all her emails. I trust and care about myself. I reconnected with family and friends, I have a beautiful relationship, and I'm part of the amazing B-School community. I'm out of debt and I'm working on my photography—my passion and my business.

I'm not afraid of failure and mistakes, I learn from them and I keep going. I take small steps, one at a time. Learning is my favorite part of life now. When in doubt, I think of Marie and I hear her saying, "Keep going, Ula—EVERYTHING IS FIGURE-OUTABLE!" I trust her immensely. She is the best role model there is. She has my back and I'm never alone.

I now understand that mistakes and failures are part of life. That we are students for life. I was in a loop of self-doubt and

(continued)

self-hate, so afraid to fail. When I watched *MarieTV*, each time I REALLY, REALLY felt like the episode was made just for me. It reached me, deep. I began to trust. Slowly, I started changing my behavior. Exercise, healthy diet, meditation. I kept going and kept learning—one step at a time. It works! I love life and I'm grateful I'm here.

—ULA
THE NETHERLANDS

9

Refuse to Be Refused

You just can't beat the person who never gives up.
Babe Ruth

Years ago, I was in a really tough spot. My business was going great, but my relationship with Josh, my beloved, was on the rocks. So much so that we were in couple's therapy. Most people don't do couple's therapy unless it's serious, which in our case, it was. One of the biggest issues on the table was how much time I spent working.

Here's the truth. I love what I do—it's part of my DNA. It's creative and exciting and fulfilling and it's a huge reason why I believe I'm on this earth. This was a hard issue for me to face, but there was indisputable evidence I couldn't deny. At that time Josh and I had been together for seven years and not once had we taken a vacation together. Yes, we traveled, but it was always work related: speaking engagements, conferences, and workshops. I sat in our therapist's office feeling angry, scared, and conflicted. From my point of view, one of the things I loved—my career—was threatening the relationship with the man I loved.

One afternoon, I came up with what I thought was a brilliant idea. What if, for his birthday, we took a vacation? A real, nonworking couple's vacation?! I looked at our calendars. Between both our schedules, there was only one little four-day window of time that this birthday vacation could happen. That it *needed* to happen. I went online and researched possibilities. I booked us a quick but exciting trip to Barcelona. It's a place Josh had talked about going for years (seven, to be precise), and yet had never visited. And we were finally at a financial place where we could make it happen.

The day of our vacation arrived. As usual, I had a full schedule with non-movable coaching calls that went right up until the moment we needed to leave. According to my calculations, we'd get to the airport right on time. The second I finished work, we hopped in a taxi and zoomed off to JFK. As it always happens when you're tight on time, we hit major traffic. I started to sweat, but even with the delay, I figured we were still fine. We jumped out, passports in hand, dragging our luggage up to the ticket counter to check in.

"Hi there, we're here to check in for the 5:45 p.m. flight to Barcelona please . . ."

The woman behind the counter took our passports and clicked away on her keyboard. She scrunched up her face, looked at her watch, pulled over a colleague to show him the screen, then looked back at her watch and said, "I'm sorry, Ms. Forleo, but there's no way you're making it on the 5:45 p.m."

"What are you talking about?! The flight hasn't left yet. It's only 4:50."

She said, "I'm sorry, but you *just* missed the deadline to check your bags. Unfortunately, I can't put you on tomorrow's flight because that's completely full, but I can put you on one that departs in two days."

"TWO DAYS? That's almost our entire trip!" *No no no no no no no.*

"Please, we have to get on *that* plane tonight. There's got to be something you can do."

"I'm sorry, for international flights, you must check your bags at least one full hour before departure. And your gate has changed so the flight is now departing from another terminal. **I'm really sorry, but you're not going to make it.**"

Time froze. My heart sank. My eyes filled with tears.

Those words "you're not going to make it" were about a lot more than the flight. I looked over and saw the disappointment on Josh's face. Not just about the trip. About us. I stood there for a moment in disbelief. Then something clicked inside of me. The deeper, wiser part of me remembered who I really am.

Everything Is Figureoutable

Everything Is Figureoutable

Everything Is Figureoutable!

I turned to Josh and said, "Get our boarding passes, I know we can figure this out." Immediately to my right was a staircase that led down to the shopping concourse. I ran down the stairs and the very first thing I saw was a luggage store. I dashed in and told the store clerk, "Real quick—I need your biggest piece of carry-on luggage and I need it NOW."

Within three minutes, I was running back up the stairs with a brand-new duffel bag.

Josh had our boarding passes. In the middle of the terminal, we started taking everything out of our big suitcase and jamming as much as we could into our new carry-on. Our frenzy was causing a bit of commotion. Understandably, two airport attendants came over to ask what we were doing.

"We REALLY need to catch this flight. We missed the deadline to check our bag so the only shot we have is if we carry on our luggage."

"Well, you can't just leave an empty suitcase in the middle of an airport. That could cause a major security lockdown," one of them said matter-of-factly. Josh, who's one of the best problem-solvers, said, "You keep packing, let me handle this." And he did.

In the meantime, I got everything I could into that duffel bag. This thing was stuffed like a friggin' sausage. We started running to the AirTrain because, remember, our flight was now departing from a whole other terminal. We got on the AirTrain at 5:20 p.m. We were three stops away from where we needed to be. Now I was a nervous wreck. I tried to stay positive, but I had to admit, this was not looking good. We got to our terminal at about 5:30 p.m., which meant we had fifteen minutes left, but we still needed to get through security and to our gate.

The AirTrain doors opened and my heart sank again. It dumped us off in some weird parking lot that we had to cross to even get *into* the terminal. Of course, walking in front of us, at a snail's pace, was a swarm of seven-year-old soccer players and their parents. I looked at Josh and said, "If these soccer-playing Smurfs get to that security line before we do, we're toast." So Josh and I picked up our overstuffed sausage (which was at least forty pounds and had no wheels) and started running around the swarm of seven-year-old soccer players and made it to the front of the security line.

At this point, it's 5:35 p.m.—ten minutes before takeoff. We took off our shoes and loaded everything onto the conveyor belt as fast as we could. We were about to walk through the metal detector when a sweet, older TSA security guard stepped in front of us, held his hands up, and said, "Whoa, whoa, whoa . . . hold on a second here." He looked Josh up and down with a suspicious, confused stare and said, "Aren't you that *guy*?!? Yeah. Yeah, man. You're that guy from TV. I've seen you on *Law and Order*. Hey, Joey—Joey! C'mere a sec. It's *that guy* on TV. You gotta meet him."

My head was about to explode. Josh replied kindly, "Yes, that's me. Thank you so much. I don't mean to be rude, but we have less than ten minutes to make our flight."

We were through security and it was almost 5:40 p.m. We still had to get to the gate. We checked our tickets and of course, *of course* our gate was the farthest one away and the terminal appeared to be at least a half mile long. I said to Josh, "Take your backpack and run. Do not let that plane leave without us. I'll be behind you—going as fast as I can."

Josh grabbed his backpack and took off down the long corridor. I summoned all my strength, picked up our forty-pound overstuffed-sausage-luggage in both hands, and started to run. Within seconds, I was sweating like a pig. Then I started to cry. Snot was streaming out of my nose and I couldn't wipe my face because I couldn't let go of the sausage-luggage. My legs were on fire and my heart felt like it was about to burst out of my chest. I started praying to God and baby Jesus and Mary: "Please, oh Lord . . . give me strength! Keep these legs going—please keep me goooooooing!!"

I turned a corner, and way off in the distance, I saw a tiny figure jumping up and down, waving his arms over his head. It was Josh! I cried even harder because I couldn't tell if he was telling me to stop or keep going. So I kept going, and going and going and going. Finally, I made it about thirty feet from the gate. Josh and the flight attendant ran up to me, grabbed the sausage-luggage, and the attendant comforted me, saying, "It's okay—you're okay, miss. You made it. Just breathe." We stumbled onto the plane in a daze, sweaty and disheveled. We shoved our sausage-luggage into the overhead bin and collapsed into our seats.

I grabbed Josh's hand, looked at him, and said, "Babe, we're going to make it. I really think we're going to make it." We took a deep breath and fastened our seat belts, when the captain came over the loudspeaker.

"Good evening, ladies and gentlemen, welcome aboard flight 1125. Unfortunately, due to some severely high winds, air traffic control is keeping us here at the gate. It doesn't look like we'll be able to take off for at least another hour. So just sit back, relax, and we'll get on our way as soon as we can."

One missed connecting flight, one rental car, and seven hours of driving through Spain later, eventually we made it to Barcelona.

Obviously, this is a personal story about doing whatever I could to save my relationship. But the point is this: Sometimes, figuring things out requires that you refuse to be refused. Just because someone else— a parent, teacher, critic, friend, loved one, flight attendant, coworker, boss, culture, or society—says, "No, you can't" or "No, that's not possible" or "No, that's not how it's done around here," doesn't mean you must agree with their version of reality.

You won't always be victorious, but you never know what's truly possible unless you try. Make it a habit to question the rules. Who can predict what strengths, capabilities, or perspectives you'll develop when you refuse to be refused? This is a practice that must be repeated again and again and again, in both small and monumental ways. Making lasting change in any aspect of our lives, or culture, is a long-term game.

Millions of scientists face years, often decades, of "failed" experiments on the path to groundbreaking discoveries. Students make countless spelling errors, mathematical miscalculations, and mistakes as they stretch to grow and learn. Artists and athletes spend years grappling with rejection and defeat in pursuit of greatness. In the United States, LGBTQ+ activists suffered countless painful losses before the Supreme Court finally ruled same-sex marriage a constitutional right. Especially when it comes to issues of social equality, we've still got a very long road ahead.

From the personal to the global, if solving a problem is that important to you, don't give up too quickly. As Margaret Thatcher reportedly said, "You may have to fight a battle more than once to win it."

HOW TO END A WAR: "WE REFUSED TO GO AWAY"

Reality is something you rise above.
Liza Minnelli

A young woman named Leymah Gbowee was born in 1972 in Monrovia, Liberia. At the time, it was one of West Africa's most vibrant and sophisticated cities. Growing up, she wanted to be a doctor. But soon after high school, a brutal civil war erupted. Leymah and her family were forced to flee to a refugee camp in Ghana, where her life became one of constant chaos, fear, and unimaginable suffering. Leymah found her way back to Monrovia when the fighting subsided in 1991, but a few years later, she gave birth to a son and found herself trapped in a nightmare of domestic abuse.

The war had taken an enormous toll on all Liberian families, but especially young women and children. Both rebels and government soldiers used rape and murder as weapons. Leymah trained to become a trauma counselor working with former child soldiers, the first of many powerful steps she used to turn her agony into action. She vowed to rebuild her life and find a way to create a better future for herself, her family, and her community.

In 1999—nearly a decade after the first civil war began—a second war started. Life grew unbearable. Again. Her abusive partner was out of the picture, but Leymah still confronted unthinkable horrors. Trucks full of armed men. Children seized in broad daylight and forced to fight. Her neighbors carried the wounded in wheelbarrows to makeshift clinics. At the sound of approaching fighters, Leymah and her family would run inside in terror. In her outstanding book, *Mighty Be Our Powers,* she recalls, "The boys, in their bandanas and oversized jeans, just passed through the cluster of homes, cradling their guns while they looked us up and down and leered. *'One of these days we'll be back to fuck you.'*"

Leymah began a deep study in the field of peace-building, focusing on the philosophies of Jesus, Martin Luther King Jr., and Gandhi. Determination and anger replaced hopelessness. In 2003, she helped organize and lead the Liberian Mass Action for Peace, where thousands of Christian and Muslim women came together to march for the cause. They wore white T-shirts and white hair ties, sitting in public protest in the town's open field. Their message was simple and clear: **We demand peace.**

They had seen the worst of humanity and they worked tirelessly, deploying any strategy or tactic they could imagine, including a sex strike, which helped garner much-needed international press and support. Day after day, week after week, the women gathered at the field and sat in protest. Leymah writes of their time in the Monrovia field (bolding is mine):

Dawn to dusk in the heat. It's one thing to go about your business on a very hot day and another to sit, unmoving, while the sun bakes you. It was a kind of torture. I turned as black as I've ever been, and many of the women broke out in terrible rashes. But there was something compelling in the pain, too: your body was being beaten, **but you were doing it for a reason,** . . . From dawn to dusk in the rain. Liberia is one of the wettest countries on earth and the water comes down on you with the strength of a fireman's hose. We sat wretched as the flood sank into the field's sandy dirt. . . .

Every day we were on that field. *Every day.* **We refused to go away.** Refused to let our suffering remain invisible. **If people didn't take us seriously at first, it was our persistence that wore them down.**

Eventually, Leymah and her peace protesters were granted a meeting with Liberia's president, Charles Taylor. While at first the meeting felt like a sign of progress, nothing changed. The violence got worse. One day, after yet another round of bombing and savage murders, something in Leymah broke. She felt a rage rise within her unlike anything she'd ever felt. Channeling that explosive energy into action, she organized hundreds more Christian and Muslim women to travel to Ghana. They surrounded the hotel where the latest round of peace negotiations had stalled. Waiting until lunchtime, nearly two hundred women stormed into the building and formed a human barricade, preventing the men from leaving until they reached a peace agreement.

Security tried to arrest Leymah, but she had another trick up her sleeve. She threatened to take off her clothes. According to traditional beliefs, this gesture would have brought a curse upon the men. And it worked. Within weeks, the Liberian war ended. President Taylor went into exile, and Leymah's courage paved the way for Africa's first female head of state, Ellen Johnson Sirleaf. In 2011, Leymah was awarded the Nobel Peace Prize for her help ending the civil war in Liberia.

Among countless lessons of unfathomable strength, tenacity, bravery, commitment, resilience, creativity, and determination, Leymah's story illustrates the otherworldly power that comes from a willingness to do whatever it takes. To figure it out no matter what. To refuse to be refused. We see the miracles that can unfold when one person is willing to risk it all and stop at nothing. These heroic women ended a war.

In case you skimmed past that last sentence, let me repeat it: These heroic women *ended a war*. They did this with no artillery. No "official" political power. No violence. If that doesn't prove that everything really is figureoutable, I don't know what does. Leymah said, "I believe, I *know*, that if you have unshakable faith in yourself, in your sisters and in the possibility of change, you can do almost anything."

DECLINING DEFEAT

If you don't risk anything, you risk even more.
Erica Jong

We have a practice in our company called doing a stress log. It's a simple exercise of making a written list of recurring stressors. The goal then is to work through that list and design systems and solutions to eliminate or transform the sources of stress, as best we can. (We have a *MarieTV* episode about this—search *Marie Forleo + stress log* online.) At one point, our management team did a collective stress log and realized that a significant stress point in our business was booking locations to shoot *MarieTV*. Every time we wanted to film more episodes, we'd have to find and rent a studio, build our sets, then break everything down and store our production equipment until the next shoot. As a virtual company, it was becoming a sizable drain on our time and resources. We decided that getting our own studio would not only alleviate that stress but create expanded opportunities to make better work.

Since I already lived in New York City, I was aware of how difficult and expensive this solution was likely to be. I had no previous experience renting commercial real estate, nor did I know anyone who did. But it's all figureoutable, so we dove in. We found a commercial real estate agent and started looking at spaces. My concerns were quickly confirmed: There weren't many options within our budget. The spaces I did see were dingy and overpriced. I stayed on the hunt, visiting dozens of unworkable spaces week after week. We were beginning to lose hope.

Then one day, I got an email about a new space. The pictures looked good—real good—and it was walking distance from my apartment. Best of all, it was around the corner from my favorite karaoke joint. When I arrived at the building with my broker, something in my body screamed, *Yesssss!! This is it—this is where you're supposed to be.* The building's super, an affable guy named Patrick, gave us a tour. I could picture our team shooting in this space and was feeling more and more excited by the minute. Amid my enthusiasm, Patrick warned me that several other companies were also interested in leasing this space.

As soon as we left, I told my broker to put in a strong offer. I could feel it in my bones that *this* was our spot. That was a Friday morning. Days and days went by. Nothing. Now, understand, the Manhattan commercial real estate market moves fast. Hearing nothing for several days was not a positive sign. In the middle of the following week, I finally got word from my agent. The owner rejected my offer and chose a tech company instead and they were already negotiating their contract. It was a done deal. I lost. I needed to move on.

But I couldn't. Something inside of me couldn't let it go. I got curious. I asked my broker why I was rejected. Why did I lose out to the tech startup? What about our offer could have been improved? Sheepishly, he confessed that my offer was fine, but the building owner didn't fully understand what my company did. Apparently, he also didn't believe I had a "stable" business (mind you, I didn't yet disclose my financials, which were solid as a rock). I was told that the tech dudes gave him more "confidence." When I heard that, Jersey Marie (my alter ego) said, "Oh *hell* no. This ain't how this is going down." So I decided to write a letter to the owner clearly detailing my company's thirteen-year history, our mission, who we serve, the results we help people create, and a detailed plan of how we intended to use the space. I poured every ounce of my heart, intelligence, and persuasive energy into that letter. I went back to the building to hand deliver it.

When I arrived, Patrick was standing outside. He greeted me with a warm but surprised-to-see-you smile.

"I'm not sure if you remember me, but I came with my broker to see the available office last Friday. I really want the space, but I heard the owner is already negotiating with a tech startup. I wrote this letter and need to get it to him before they close the deal. Can you help me?"

"Uhh. He's not here right now." Clearly, I caught Patrick off guard and my directness was making him a little uncomfortable.

"Please, Patrick. I know you must have his number. Can you call him real fast? Right now? It won't take more than two minutes. It's really important that I get this letter to him as quickly as I can. You're the *only* chance I've got."

He reluctantly took out his phone and called the owner. I stood there as Patrick awkwardly tried to explain that some random woman needed to get him a very important letter, ASAP. Judging by the backpedaling Patrick had to do, it was apparent that the owner was not happy with this out-of-the-blue phone call.

Nevertheless, Patrick took my letter and agreed to pass it along. I thanked him again for his help and walked away. Four more days go by. Still no response. Now it's the weekend. I resigned myself to the fact that I lost that battle. Even though I was disappointed, I also felt a sense of satisfaction with my effort. I'd gone the extra mile and done everything I could. I had faith that there must be an even better space out there and resolved to do whatever it took to find it. On Monday morning, I woke up to this email from my broker:

Hi Marie,

I was just contacted by the owner's agent. The owner had a chance to read your letter and would like to meet with you. I am not privy to any breakdowns with the current negotiations but this is great news for us as it likely means that there is an opening . . . LET'S CAPITALIZE ON THIS OPPORTUNITY!

B A M!

I immediately set up an in-person meeting. Turns out, that tech company wasn't as "stable" as they first thought. I rolled in with an open heart, enthusiasm, bulletproof financials, and a promise to respect and care for the space. Long story short, we got it.

That experience proved to be a real turning point for our team. Not only did we solve an exhausting stress point, but our studio has become a place of joy, creation, and transformative work. We've used it to film hundreds of *MarieTV* episodes, podcasts, live streams, webinars, and training programs. It's allowed us to think bigger and create work in a way that just wasn't possible before. Patrick has also become one of our most beloved colleagues.

Even though I know it's important to be persistent in the face of resistance (heck, I'm teaching you about it right now!), it's still a habit I work on. To this day, I still have to bat down the voice in my head that says things like, "You can't do *that*—that's too much, Marie." And, "You're being too _____."

direct
demanding
aggressive
expressive
pushy
controlling
out-there
loud
raw
raunchy
wacky
emotional
etc.

Thankfully, the wiser part of me (*ahem*, Jersey Marie) often pipes up and prevails. Her favorite response is, "Pfft! Forget *all* that shit. Go for what you want."

While I believe everyone should question the rules and challenge the status quo, this is especially crucial for women. We're battling a culture that's worked to shame, silence, and control us for millennia. Many of us have been conditioned since birth to suppress our desires, curtail our strengths, hide our power, deny our emotions, and be "nice."

But you weren't built to be contained. You're here to create, to heal, and to make change. Never apologize for that. You can't make a difference without making waves.

THANK YOU FOR NOT BELIEVING IN ME

In every position that I've been in, there have been naysayers who don't believe I'm qualified or who don't believe I can do the work. And I feel a special responsibility to prove them wrong.

Sonia Sotomayor

As an artist, you need the naysayers and the nonbelievers to add fuel to your creative fire.

Ice-T

Have you ever had someone say something horrible about your goal, project, or idea? Where their words hit you like a punch in the gut and left you thinking, "How could someone be *that* mean?" I have. Many times. It continues to happen to this day.

When you're blazing new trails and making change—expect a steady stream of criticism, judgment, and even ridicule. It can come from your own mind, your loved ones, friends, mentors, colleagues, total strangers, and rando ass-biscuits on the internet. It's important to realize that (A) this is normal, (B) you're more than capable of handling it, and (C) sometimes a put-down can be the best fuel to fire you up.

Let me tell you about an interesting encounter I had at a big business conference. My flagship program, B-School, was a few months away from launching for the very first time. I was bright-eyed and excited about meeting new people and learning new ideas. My conference badge was hanging around my neck. I held tight to my big plastic binder. I was committed to finding promotional partners and doing everything in my power to get the word out about my new course.

On the first day of the event, I was in the hotel heading up to the main ballroom on an escalator when this guy—also an attendee at that conference—introduced himself and asked about my business. I was thrilled to share. I told him about my new program and its mission to give creatives and small-business owners the skills they needed to market and sell with integrity online. I said that business education could be enjoyable, heart-centered, and even fun, while still generating massive results.

He laughed and said, "Really? Is that a *real* business? You actually make money doing that? C'mon now. This is a hobby, isn't it? Tell the truth. You've got a rich boyfriend or husband who pays your bills."

For a few long seconds, I was speechless. Was this dickwad serious? Was I caught in some nightmarish time-machine? Because last I checked, it was 2009 not 1909. My blood boiled. It took restraint to keep from grabbing him by the collar and throwing him off that damn escalator.

While it stung in the moment, the truth is I'm grateful for that interaction. I thank him for not believing in me or my idea. Why? Because his words fueled me to make B-School an even bigger success. His blatant ignorance reaffirmed how important my mission was to help business owners (especially women) control their financial destinies. I hustled even harder at that conference. I was already committed but, after that exchange, absolutely nothing was going to stop me.

When people shit on your dreams, become an alchemist who turns negativity into productive gold. Bullshit makes good fertilizer. Fuck-you fuel, if you will. Yes, I'm aware that wanting to prove people wrong isn't a healthy source of long-term motivation. But in the moment, we work with what we've got. Refusing to be refused means taking a stand for yourself and protecting your dreams.

To be clear, this isn't about being so sensitive that you don't seek the critical input needed to learn, grow, and improve. There's a difference between getting defensive and getting determined. This is about maturity, discernment, and most crucially, considering your source.

NOT ALL CRITICISM IS CREATED EQUAL

Haters are confused admirers who can't understand why everybody else likes you.

Paulo Coelho

As long as there is creativity, there will be criticism of it.

After sharing my work publicly for two decades, I'm intimately familiar with the hate and negativity folks can throw your way. I've also received thousands of questions from readers about how to deal with the fear of criticism. Any of this sound familiar?

I'm so fearful of criticism and judgment that it keeps me from putting my ideas out there. I have trouble separating my work from my sense of self.

I'm afraid people will discover I'm a fraud and that I don't really know what I'm doing.

I know everyone is entitled to their own opinions, but how do you not let it
     affect you in a negative and hurtful way?
Marie, how do YOU deal with criticism—you put yourself out there all
     the time!

As the adage goes, "To avoid criticism, say nothing, do nothing, be nothing." But even that's not the full picture. Because those who do nothing are also criticized; they're judged harshly for being lazy good-for-nothings. Realize that criticism and judgment are a natural part of life. Don't resist that fact, embrace it.

Fact: You're already being judged right now.

It's true. Strangers judge you. People who barely know you judge you. People who genuinely love you judge you. They judge how you look. They judge what you're choosing to do or not do with your life. They judge what you eat and don't eat. People judge the clothes you wear, what music you listen to, your politics, personal beliefs, how you spend your money, how you raise your kids, what car you drive, where you live, who you worship, and who you love.

If you're honest, you judge yourself, too. You say some mean stuff to yourself on the regular (you're too slow, too old, too young, too fat, too insecure, too shy, too _____). You also judge and criticize others, even when you don't intend to. Human beings are judging machines. Our judgments are often biased and wildly inaccurate. So what? The trick is to have a sense of humor about it. Don't personalize it, dwell on it, or indulge in it.

Fact: Everything you love is despised by someone else.

> I went for years not finishing anything. Because, of course, when you finish something you can be judged.
>
> *Erica Jong*

For every single thing you think is extraordinary in this world—every movie, book, food item, comedian, TV show—guess what? Someone else hates it. Which is why most criticism is not constructive or even worth listening to. It's just someone's opinion. You know what they say about those, right? Opinions are like assholes; everyone has one and most of them stink.

Let's say you love chocolate, but you have a friend who despises chocolate. Does that mean chocolate sucks? No. It means one person doesn't like chocolate. Chocolate makers don't lose sleep over that. They're not campaigning to convert the haters. They focus all their attention on chocolate lovers.

Seth Godin pointed out that twelve percent of the more than twenty-one thousand book reviews for *Harry Potter and the Sorcerer's Stone* gave it one or two stars on Amazon.[1] That means at least 2,500 people believe that this global phenomenon sucks dong. Do you think J. K. Rowling cries in her teacup over harsh reviews? Doubtful. She's too busy inspiring (and making) billions with her art.

Everyone has a right to their opinion. But opinions are subjective. Just because someone doesn't like what you do doesn't mean no one else will. A person's opinion is not The Truth. It's *their* truth. It's unwise to waste time and emotional energy over the criticism of folks you don't know, respect, or serve.

My work certainly isn't for everyone. It's only for creative badasses, like you.

Fact: The more you care about what others think, the more they own you.

It's not your job to like me, it's mine.
Byron Katie

Why should the way you feel depend on the thoughts in someone else's head?

Never give anyone the power to control your emotions. Not your parents. Not your spouse. Not your siblings or friends or coworkers or even your kids. Definitely not your politicians. And *especially* not randos on the internet. Realize that people can say whatever they want, but you do not have to take it in or give the power to ruin your day. Eleanor Roosevelt said it best: "No one can make you feel inferior without your consent."

Your time on this planet is precious. YOU are precious. Think about it this way: Would you allow someone to walk into your house, squat in your living room, and take a hot, steaming dump on your rug, and then walk out, leaving you to clean it up? I hope not. When you hear nasty, baseless criticism, reject it. Refuse it. Say, "Nope. You can't take me down. I won't give you that power. I don't allow anyone to take a shit in my living room."

Fact: Use what helps, leave the rest.

When it comes to critical feedback, don't be *so* fragile that you miss out on information that can help you learn and improve. Be strong enough to extract the value from the critics, if it's there. These questions help:

"What could be true about this?"
"Is there any part that I can use to grow and do better?"

Supportive and caring folks usually share advice with you in private, *after* you've asked for their input. Even then, they do so in a way that supports your growth, not stunts it. The people closest to me do that. I'm grateful they look out for me, and I work hard to do the same for them.

THREE TACTICS TO PRACTICE

1. ALWAYS CONSIDER THE SOURCE

I've never received a piece of hurtful, vitriolic criticism from anyone I admire or respect. Most successful people don't have time to harshly criticize others because they're too busy making change and living their lives.

The harshest critics are often insecure, unaccomplished cowards. They're bystanders on the sidelines of life who risk nothing and create nothing. As novelist Chuck Palahniuk says, "It's easy to attack and destroy an act of creation. It's a lot more difficult to perform one." Remember to take a step back and consider the source. Does the person criticizing you have a body of work you respect? Are they someone you genuinely admire? If not, think carefully before taking their opinion to heart.

2. FEEL SAD, NOT MAD

Imagine how painful and miserable someone's life must be to have time to be *that* mean. When people tear others down, they're broadcasting the following about themselves:

- They have very little empathy, compassion, and emotional intelligence.
- They've got too much time on their hands, which means they're underperforming.
- They're starved for attention.
- Their lives are filled with hurt and pain.

Feel sad for them, not mad. And definitely don't use their attacks to shape your creations.

3. HAVE A GOOD LAUGH

Here's a screenshot of folks having a very spirited, detailed discussion about what they believe to be one of the most important, consequential aspects of my work:

Does anyone know how much of Marie's hair is false? I'd guess that mane she tossed over her shoulders is 70% extensions.

marielaporte: Ding! Ding! Ding!

I'd go with around 80% actually. I've always found her gobs of fake hair very distracting. And I've been surprised to see her being praised for her great hair when it's obviously almost entirely extensions. Her natural hair is just the layers around her face—I've never seen it longer than slightly past her shoulders.

Her natural hair is not thick at all. She covers this up with teasing the hair close to her scalp as much as possible to make her hair look fuller. (This is obvious even in the pics without the extensions.)

News flash, haters: It's all my natural hair.

It sucks that people spend time and energy tearing each other down, especially about their looks, but we've decided to make jokes about the "realness" of my hair on my show. While of course I've gotten harsher criticism, it's way more fun to shine a light on the pettiness of internet trolls and nullify their nastiness with laughs.*

---

*Obviously, online nastiness is distinct from serious threats of harm, violence, or death. If anyone ever threatens you, call law enforcement immediately.

GOLDEN RULE: Never reply when angry, emotional, or buzzed.

One night in the nascent social media era (I'm talking late 2008ish), I was scheduled to be a guest on an entrepreneurial Twitter chat, starting at 9:00 p.m. Earlier that evening, I went to a networking event where I enjoyed a glorious glass of cabernet. Once I got back to my apartment, it was time to hop on Twitter. I remember sitting at my desk, in the dark, and thinking to myself how strange it was to start working again at 9:00 p.m. The first seven minutes went smoothly. I was sharing resources, firing off pithy responses, making jokes, and having a grand old time. Until, that is, a troll hopped into our discussion.

Daytime, wine-free Marie knows better than to engage with trolls. She's usually got perspective, compassion, and self-restraint. But just one glass of cabernet was enough to throw those qualities right out the door. Jersey Marie took over and replied in her typical raw, no-holds-barred form. My taunts and comebacks, while funny to me in the moment, were mean. Not a reflection of my highest self, by a long shot. The next morning, I looked back at the thread and regretted my behavior. I made myself a promise **to never again respond** when I'm angry or overly emotional. And definitely *never* touch a keyboard if I've had even a tiny sip of wine. That was over a decade ago and I haven't broken my promise since. In our modern culture, you're writing your history one tweet, one comment, and one post at a time.

THE ULTIMATE SECRET BEHIND REFUSING TO BE REFUSED

> In a world where there is so much to be done, I felt
> strongly impressed that there must be something for
> me to do.
>
> *Dorothea Dix*

When Leymah set out to stop a war, it wasn't for personal accolades. She didn't have "Winning the Nobel Peace Prize" on her vision board. She persevered against unimaginable odds to create a better life for her family, her community, and for generations to come. When I got our studio space, it wasn't because I thought it made us look cool, but because I couldn't stand seeing my team stressed. Plus, we had tons of creative ideas to better serve our audience, and I knew a dedicated space would help us deliver on our mission. Remember how fired up I was after encountering Mr. Dickwad on the escalator? That wasn't just about me. I felt a responsibility to kick ass on behalf of women who've been underestimated *everywhere*. Even at JFK, the underlying motivation that fueled me wasn't about a vacation—it was about my devotion to Josh, our love, and our relationship.

Want to supercharge your ability to persevere, no matter what setbacks or obstacles get in your way? Make sure your dream is tied to something beyond yourself. Striving to be your best is one thing, but when you do your best for the betterment of others, you'll be virtually unstoppable. A bigger, more expansive purpose beyond our own personal gain is what gives our lives meaning. Purpose fuels persistence. Motives matter.

If your dreams are only about personal gain—fame, money, or power—

you'll eventually run out of steam. Even if you do manage to reach your goal, the win will feel shallow. You'll wonder, *Is that it? Is this really all there is?*

The measure of our lives is not determined by what we achieve for ourselves; it's determined by what we share, give, and contribute to others. When your dreams are connected to a sense of contribution beyond yourself—a family member, your coworkers, or a community or cause you deeply believe in—you'll unlock wellsprings of strength, stamina, and courage you never knew you had. Most important, you'll experience a greater sense of meaning and fulfillment, too.

To be clear, having dreams for yourself is awesome. We all start there. Just don't stop there. Connect your dream to a greater good. It'll feed your soul and provide the emotional strength you'll need to refuse to be refused.

INSIGHT TO ACTION CHALLENGE

We can do anything we want to do if we stick to it long enough.

Helen Keller

Just don't give up trying to do what you really want to do. If there is love and inspiration, I don't think you can go wrong.

Ella Fitzgerald

1. *What's at least one example of a time when you've refused to be refused and, in doing so, found a way around a limitation?* No example is too small or insignificant. List as many as you can think of and what you learned by refusing to be refused.

2. *Have you already been refused on the path to your big dream?* What did you do? Revisit that refusal and brainstorm seven ways you can work around it and keep going!

3. *What positive results might occur if you challenged authority, questioned the rules, or declined defeat just 10 percent more than you currently do?*

4. *Imagine the criticism you fear actually happens.* What are three constructive and healthy ways you could deal with it? How would

your highest and best self respond—if at all? Feel free to adopt my rule of never replying in anger (or after you've had wine). A clear-headed plan now prevents pain and regret later.

5. *Write down ten things you would do if you had absolutely zero fear of judgment or criticism.* Then pick one and do it.

6. *How can you connect your dream or goal to something beyond yourself?* Is there a family member, community, or cause you can serve? Reasons power results.

Figureoutable Field Notes

After getting rejected from fourteen care facilities, everything is figureoutable *helped her find an outstanding facility for her brother, who suffers from early-onset Alzheimer's.*

My sweet brother Craig has early-onset Alzheimer's and had become agitated and sometimes violent in his assisted living situation. It was up to me to find a new care facility with appropriate services for him.

I flew to Ohio from my home in Mexico, expecting to spend a week. It took a month.

I visited over thirty facilities, got declined by fourteen, hospitalized him to stabilize his medications, all while coordinating communication among social workers and doctors.

That idea and mantra "Everything is figureoutable" helped me to persist, to research, to explore, and to keep the crippling feeling of helplessness out of my world. I followed up with everyone in person rather than on the phone or through emails. Every time I heard, "No," I asked for their suggestions. I asked everyone for ideas and referrals and thanked them all in person, in addition to sending emails expressing my appreciation. I kept my emotions in check so my brain could work. I owe much of that ability to repeating to myself, "Everything is figureoutable."

(continued)

The best facility in the area said they had a six-month wait list for transfer patients. I was disappointed, but determined to get my brother admitted. I used every reason I could think of to keep reconnecting with the admissions officer. I stopped by to make sure he received my paperwork. I dropped in again a few days later to ask what number we were on the wait list.

After my brother needed a medication adjustment, I stopped by again to let the admissions officer know, and asked again about the wait list. They told me they had a newly open bed, which my brother was potentially eligible for.

The next day, as I was leaving the hospital, I got the magic call. Yes! My sweet brother had his bed waiting for him in the best Alzheimer's nursing home in the region! My brother is now receiving the best possible care available to him in an outstanding facility. I am at peace, knowing this is true.

—JANET
MEXICO

10

The World Needs Your Special Gift

There is a vitality, a life force, a quickening that is translated through you into action, and because there is only one of you in all time, this expression is unique, and if you block it, it will never exist through any other medium, and be lost. The world will not have it. It is not your business to determine how good it is, not how it compares with other expression. It is your business to keep it yours clearly and directly, to keep the channel open.

Martha Graham

Early in our relationship, Josh would leave town for work and return home only to find empty cans of Chef Boyardee and boxes of Kraft Mac & Cheese stuffed in our trash. He'd offer me vitamin supplements and suggest that we start "juicing."

Whatever, hippie man. I'm working, like, four jobs right now. I have zero extra cash. I ain't got time to learn your granola-loving ways. He was persistently kind and I was persistently stubborn. *I don't want to. It's too expensive. Too weird. Just, no. Pass the mac and cheese please.*

A few years later, I became friends with Kris Carr, a cancer-thriver and wellness icon who touted the benefits of juicing, superfoods, and a plant-based diet. "Josh! OMG, I met this *amazing* woman. She's a total badass who's written all these bestselling health books—check out these recipes for smoothies and green juices and salads. Here's the juicer we need to get and, oh yeah, she said we should take these supplements. You know, we really should have started this years ago."

A justified face-palm moment for Josh.

"Marie, you've got to be kidding me. I've been telling you the exact same thing for years now. Why couldn't you hear it from me?!"

And that's the point.

One of the biggest obstacles to figuring out your dream is this: You incorrectly assume that "it's all been done before." You don't believe you have anything original, valuable, or worthwhile to contribute. You don't feel special or talented enough to add your voice to the mix.

It's time to set the record straight.

No matter how many times you think an idea or creation has been shared in the world, sometimes it takes that *one* person expressing it in their unique voice, at the right time, in the right place, for it to actually make a difference.

YOU are that person for somebody.

It doesn't matter how many people have gone before you. It doesn't matter how many versions of the same thing you think already exist or have been done by more talented, qualified, or famous people. Forget all that. With over 7.7 BILLION people on the planet (and counting!), there are more than enough humans with a diverse set of needs, perspectives, problems, preferences, desires, and tastes. There's always room for more. There's always room for you.

YOU ARE HERE FOR A REASON

> Every individual matters. Every individual has a role to play. Every individual makes a difference.
>
> *Jane Goodall*

God, Source, Smurf Fairies—whatever form of higher intelligence you might believe in—did not make any extra people just for the heck of it. No other person has, or ever will have, the unique blend of talents, strengths, perspective, and gifts that you have. Remember, you are a onetime mega event in the universe.

Don't fucking waste it.

You were born with an innate power to create change, both in your life and in the lives of others. This power doesn't exist outside of yourself, and it's not something you can buy or borrow. You already have it within you, *right now*.

I believe that inner power led you to this book. The whole reason you're here reading, right now, is because you want to bring some *thing* to life.

That said, here's what's vital to understand. When you have an idea, a possibility, the tiniest nugget of a dream for yourself or others and you don't do everything you can to bring it to life . . .

YOU ARE STEALING FROM THOSE
WHO NEED YOU MOST.

That's right, I said . . .

Stealing.

There are countless people out there who need the gifts that you and you alone are here to give. If you don't get off your ass and do the things your heart keeps telling you to do, the world will have lost something truly irreplaceable . . .

YOU.

It will have lost your unique voice. Your unique energy. Your unique ideas and stories and perspective. By holding back and playing small, you're robbing countless people of the goodness and joy and healing and growth that *only* your unique contributions can offer.

Maybe you're stealing from future customers or fans who are waiting for the exact kind of _____ [book, song, story, movie, novel, stand-up routine, speech, nonprofit, educational platform, pasta dish, T-shirt, app, etc.] you've been dreaming of.

Maybe you're stealing from your kids, loved ones, or colleagues because they're not getting the real you—the most fully alive, emotionally available, playful, confident, strong, and loving you that you could be. Maybe you're stealing from generations to come because you're not willing to heal a wound or break a cycle that must be broken in order for others to have a better life.

When any of us deny or suppress or minimize our gifts, those gifts sour into a toxic poison. That poison eats us alive from the inside out. We become sick, lethargic, bitter, cynical, angry, addicted, short-tempered, and judgmental—and that's just for starters. Never forget, Hitler was a frustrated artist.

> If you bring forth what is within you, what you bring forth will save you. If you do not bring forth what is within you, what you do not bring forth will destroy you.
>
> *Gospel of Thomas*

Consider all the things that have brought you value, joy, or growth throughout your lifetime. Every song that's made your head bop. Every movie that's made you laugh, cry, or expand your point of view. Every athlete or artist who's inspired you to reach for more. Every invention that's made your life easier. Every restaurant that's served a dish that made you moan with delight. Every book that's opened your eyes to a different world. Every teacher, mentor, neighbor, or friend whose words or actions or leadership has guided you. Any bit of technology (e.g., electricity, Wi-Fi, cameras) that's somehow enhanced your life.

Imagine if all those beautiful people never followed the call of their soul—never "figured out" their dreams and created and contributed and shared. I say this at the end of every *MarieTV* episode and I'll say it to you now:

The world needs that special gift that only you have.

It's true and you know it. You've known this since you were little. You've sensed that there's something special inside of you, something distinct and extraordinary that you, and only you, came here to create and express. Trust that feeling. It's your life force. Your genius. Your destiny screaming to be realized.

Uncovering, developing, and sharing your gifts—that's the whole reason you're here on earth. I believe that's the whole reason any of us are here! To create and contribute to one another.

To be clear, your gifts don't have to be grand in scale or epic in their reach. All contributions are necessary and valuable. Right now, your gift may be the nourishing meals you cook for friends and family. The compassion and understanding you bring to tough conversations. Your gifts may involve wood sculptures, paintings, plumbing, activism, fighting fires, making comics, producing plays, doing research, rehabilitating animals, designing eco-friendly urban spaces, designing jewelry, or coaching your daughter's Little League team.

Your gifts might be expressed through volunteer work, or through the attention, respect, and caring you show every person you meet— from your bank teller to a stranger on the street. Your gift may be the way your garden inspires hope and wonder in your neighborhood. You likely have many gifts, and those gifts will develop and evolve over the course of your life, just as you do.

"But, Marie—really—I have nothing unique to offer. It's ALL been done before."

Imagine your favorite coffee shop or clothing store (any source of joy or value—it can be a sex toy company for all I care). Now imagine the creator having the same limiting thought that you're having. Imagine her throwing her hands up in the air before she even started—*"Why even bother?!? Everyone already beat me to it. The world has enough damn caffeine/ T-shirts/dildos!"*

That would suck, right? I think about this as it relates to Italian food. One of my go-to spots is a little mom-and-pop joint called Pepe Rosso. They have one of the best eggplant parms in lower Manhattan. Imagine if the founders of Pepe Rosso, when thinking about opening their restaurant, threw their hands in the air and said, *"You know what? There's already a thousand Italian restaurants in NYC. And another thing, there's already way TOO MUCH eggplant parm in the world—fuhgeddaboudit!!!"* (The thought of never having Pepe Rosso's eggplant parm again is giving me heart palpitations.)

Keep going with any area of art, science, sports, or culture. All of the musicians in the world didn't stop Beyoncé or Lady Gaga or Stevie Nicks or Kendrick Lamar from adding their voices to the mix. The popularity of Phil Donahue didn't stop Oprah. Margaret Cho's comedic ingenuity didn't stop Ali Wong from expressing hers. Just imagine how much we would have missed out on if any of those brilliant beings stopped at the thought that their contribution was unnecessary because it had already been done. As Fred Rogers said, "If you could only sense how important you are to the lives of those you meet; how important you can be to people you may never dream of."

Yes, there are millions of books and songs and plays and businesses and hot sauce makers and knitting clubs. But if you haven't done your version yet, then no—it has *not* all been done before. Because it hasn't yet been expressed by the once-in-a-lifetime miracle that is you.

OVERCOME THE FRAUD FACTOR

What do J.Lo, Jodie Foster, and Maya Angelou have in common? It's not the fact that they're all award-winning cultural icons, it's that they've all felt like impostors. Total fakes and frauds.

> Even though I had sold 70 million albums, there I was feeling like "I'm no good at this."
>
> *Jennifer Lopez*

When I won the Oscar, I thought it was a fluke. I thought everybody would find out, and they'd take it back. Excuse me, we meant to give that to someone else. That was going to Meryl Streep.

Jodie Foster

I have written eleven books, but each time I think, "Uh oh, they're going to find out now. I've run a game on everybody, and they're going to find me out."

Maya Angelou

If you ever feel like a fraud—like any accomplishment is a fluke or mistake and someday people are going to find out—you're clearly in good company. According to research, impostor syndrome affects a whopping 70 percent of us.[1]

While feeling like a fraud is universal among humans, it tends to hit women the hardest. Why? Because as women, and members of other traditionally underrepresented groups, it's easy to look around and feel like we don't belong. Socially, we've been conditioned to self-deprecate and downplay our abilities, which leads to low self-esteem and self-sabotage that adversely affects every sphere of our lives. When we internalize that message—that we're not the real deal—we suffer major consequences. Not just emotionally or creatively, but financially. I'm talking smaller careers and smaller bank accounts.

That's why it's vital to not only acknowledge this phenomenon, but take active steps to ensure that "fraud feeling" doesn't prevent you from sharing your gifts and reaching the heights you're capable of. Here are a few steps to stop impostor syndrome before it stops you.

1. SHARE THE SHAME

Most high achievers struggle with feeling like a fake, but never talk about it. It's like a dirty little secret everyone's afraid to admit. I'll tell you right now—I still feel this way at times and I've been doing this work for almost two decades. Brené Brown says, "As a shame researcher, I know that the very best thing to do in the midst of a shame attack is totally counterintuitive: Practice courage and reach out!"[2]

Brené is on point. You know why? Because shame always shrivels when you share it out loud. It simply cannot exist when brought into the light. To take this idea even further, I recommend you put one or two trusted souls on speed dial for when that fraud festival comes to town. These folks are your new Fraud Squad—people you can connect with and say, "Hey, I'm feeling like I suck right now. Can you remind me why I don't?"

Naturally, you must return the favor. It feels good to be the person who lifts others up and reminds them of their intrinsic worth, especially when they can't see it themselves. Our world has more than enough critics. Be an encourager instead.

2. START A HYPE FILE

A hype file is a place where you stockpile compliments, thank-yous, accolades, and any comments from people who've said you've positively impacted them. Maybe it was a text from a friend, a note from a colleague, or a voicemail from a client. No kind word or display of appreciation is too small for your hype file. You can even add your accomplishments, too. Collect them in a central location and review as often as needed. Remember, where attention goes energy flows. A hype file can combat the negative effects of imposter syndrome and reground you in the reality that, yes, you are, in fact, the real deal.

3. SHINE YOUR LIGHT OUT, NOT IN

Think of your attention—your mental, emotional, and spiritual energy—as a flashlight that can only shine in one direction. In any given moment, your flashlight is either shining in on you and how much you feel like a fake OR it's shining out on others—what they need, want, and how you can help them.

When your flashlight is shining out, you're giving zero attention to your fraud feelings. Without attention, those feelings can't survive.

Shining your light on others doesn't need to be time-consuming or overly complicated, any act of kindness can do the trick. Maybe you send your boss a thank-you note detailing something specific that made a difference to you. Perhaps you offer support to a neighbor in need. You could even visit a local elderly home and find out who hasn't had any visitors lately and go make their day. Look around. There's no shortage of people hungry for a moment of connection. There's always someone who could use a little assistance. A little attention. A little comfort. A little love.

Next time you catch yourself feeling like a fraud, check yourself. Chances are, you're shining your flashlight on yourself rather than directing it where it can make its greatest impact—caring for others.

For more tips to combat the fraud feeling, search *MarieTV + imposter syndrome* online to watch the episode on this topic. If you're still not convinced that you have a right to share your special gifts, this next part should help.

LIFE-CHANGING ADVICE
FROM THE DEAD

Whatever you want to do, do it now. There are only so many tomorrows.

Attributed to Michael Landon

Bronnie Ware is a former nurse who spent years working in palliative care, caring for hundreds of patients during the last weeks of their lives. The level of frustration among some of her patients inspired her to write a book called *The Top Five Regrets of the Dying*. There's one specific regret I'd like us to focus on—the biggest, most common regret of them all.*

"I wish I'd had the courage to live a life true to myself, not the life others expected of me."

Oof. Gets you in the gut, right?

What Bronnie discovered is that at the time of their death, most people had not honored even *half* of their dreams. HALF! The point here isn't to lament other people's mistakes, but to avoid making your own.

Tell the truth. How often do you bite your tongue instead of saying

---

*The other regrets, in order, are: "I wish I hadn't worked so hard"; "I wish I'd had the courage to express my feelings"; "I wish I had stayed in touch with my friends"; and "I wish I had let myself be happier."

or doing what you really feel? What have you denied yourself the pleasure of exploring or expressing because you don't want to be judged or criticized? What are you still doing, even though you can't stand it, because you're terrified to attempt your secret dreams? How much of your life exists to gain the approval of your parents, spouse, family, children, friends, or (most tragically) strangers on the internet?

The fact that you're reading these words right now indicates you have one big advantage: you're still here, which means you still have time to change. Please, for the love of all things holy, do what you dream of now so you'll never regret not having tried. Otherwise, you might end up uttering four of the worst words any human can ever say:

"I wish I had . . ."

Those four damn words.

I wish I had . . .

Look.

Whether you realize it or not, we're all on the same cosmic train, heading to the same destination. Death. None of us knows when our stop is coming. We have no idea when the train will slow down, when the conductor will tap our shoulder and say, *"This is your stop, little lady. Time to go."*

All we know is that with every passing moment, we're getting closer. Day by day. Hour by hour. Minute by minute. That's why now is the time to go after that dream of yours, no matter how wild, unreasonable, or seemingly "impossible" it is. Now is the time to figure it all out. Everything you think and say and do from this moment on is a declaration of your commitment to that dream.

You have the power within you. You already have everything you need to answer the call of your soul. So please. Get your ass moving. Keep going. Don't steal your gifts from us.

The world really does need you. It needs your boldest, bravest, most honest and loving expression, and it needs it now. If you haven't noticed, the human race is yearning for change. You can feel it in the air. In our schools, our homes, our businesses, our sports arenas, and throughout every facet of society, people are waiting for someone to stand up and show them the way. For someone to lead with heart and with the highest vision of what we're capable of.

I believe *you* are that someone. I believe *you* are someone who can awaken a new possibility in your circle of influence, in your family, in your community, and in the world at large. I believe *you* have what it takes to figure anything out.

In doing so, you'll be an inspiration for every life you touch.

That's the opportunity. For you and for me and for the entire human race.

What we need now, more than anything else, is people like you who believe in what's possible and who live as though everything *is* figureoutable. From the environment to our food system to education to health care to inequality and injustice on every level, there are so many important things to figure out.

Throughout history, there are people who ask, "Does it really have to be this way?" or "How can we do things differently?" Even when facing social constructs that have been entrenched for centuries, the dreams of one individual have sparked change across all of society.

When we approach our personal problems and our collective challenges in this way—that everything really *is* figureoutable—it will all start to change. We'll go from feeling defeated and overwhelmed and broken to courageous and capable and full of hope.

We must teach this to ourselves and to each other and to our children and to our children's children. Because there will be moments in your life when an opportunity presents itself for you to do something, or say something, or change something.

Promise yourself that from this moment forward, you won't waste one more minute of one more day saying, "I don't know how to do that." Or "I don't know if I have what it takes to become that."

Because we both know in our heart of hearts that, yes, you do. You are divinely blessed and infinitely capable. There is no circumstance or fate or situation that can hinder the unstoppable power of your human soul.

Hopefully, we'll bump into each other on that cosmic train someday. If I'm still riding, I'll be waiting for you in the bar car. Sipping an Aperol spritz, eager to hear how it went.

INSIGHT TO ACTION
CHALLENGE

*In the long run, we shape our lives and we shape our-
selves. The process never ends until we die. And, the
choices we make are ultimately our own responsibility.*

Eleanor Roosevelt

1. ***What holds you back from going for your biggest dream or aspi-
   ration?*** Ask yourself if what worries you now will still worry you in
   twenty, forty, or sixty years. Will that concern still matter?

2. ***Imagine death is imminent. Finish the following sentence at least
   twenty times (more if needed).*** Don't overthink. Just keep writing.

   I wish I had . . .
   I wish I had . . .
   I wish I had . . .

3. ***If you believed to your core that everything really*** is ***figureoutable,
   what would you now do?*** What would you create or heal or transform or transcend? Who would you become?

4. ***Please complete this last challenge by hand. Grab a journal.
   Turn off all electronic notifications.*** Find a space where you will
   not be disturbed. Light a candle if that helps get you into a quiet,
   contemplative mood. Set an alarm for fifteen minutes. You're going

to do automatic writing, which is a practice of inviting your intuition to communicate with you on the page.

Your Future Self (*the one-hundred-plus-year-old you*) is going to write a letter to the current-day you.

Before you begin, repeat the following statement three times. "I am now receiving what is for my highest good from the highest source." Write a letter from the future you to current-day you, beginning with this prompt.

Dearest [Your First Name],
  I would love you to know that . . .

Allow your hand to move. Remember, you're inviting the one-hundred-year-old you to share wisdom with current-day you. Even if it's gibberish, keep the pen on the page. Do your best not to judge, edit, or even consciously think. Write whatever comes through and pay no attention to grammar, spelling, or punctuation. Just keep scribbling. If you get stuck, start a new line and experiment with these prompts:

  I'd love you to let go of . . .
  I'd love you to start . . .
  I'd love you to remember . . .

This is for your eyes only. Keep writing until the timer hits fifteen minutes. This future-self exercise helps you access deep truths that you know intuitively, but are likely not living or practicing consistently—yet. Set your writing aside for at least an hour before you read it.

Well done. Before our time together comes to an end, just one last thing . . .

EPILOGUE

The Real Secret to
Lasting Success

Alone we can do so little. Together we can do so much.
Helen Keller

A few years ago, I hired a film crew to record our big three-day conference in New York. We'd been planning this for nearly a year. Speakers came from across the country, and hundreds of students flew in from all over the world. Immediately after the conference, our film crew went directly to the airport. They were heading to Europe to interview a half dozen B-School grads for a series of case studies. The logistics and money required to record a three-day conference, followed by a week of international filming, would make your head spin.

After the trip, I got a call from my team. Our film crew's equipment was stolen. Every camera, every lens, every tripod, and every second of footage—the entire conference and a dozen interviews across multiple European cities. Gonzo.

I threw up in my mouth.

Not only was losing that footage creatively devastating (the conference was unrepeatable), but we had a crucial promotional campaign planned around those interviews—a promotion our company needed to survive. The campaign was weeks away. Because of how many outside partners we had on board to support it, there was no way to push back our launch date.

But here's what's wild. That sick feeling in my stomach lasted only a few moments. Why? **Because my entire team lives and breathes the figureoutable philosophy.** It's embedded in our company's culture.

During that same phone call, our head of storytelling presented a reshoot plan, complete with a revamped travel schedule and interviewee approval.

I took a deep breath and said, "All right. We can do this. It's totally figureoutable!" Within a few days, the crew got new equipment, packed up, and flew back to Europe. Yes, it was intense. Yes, we busted ass and worked around the clock. But we pulled together, leaned on each other, and got the job done on time. And guess what? The new interview footage was even better than the first round!

Anyone who leads an organization or manages a department or runs a household knows this: shit goes wrong all the time. Meltdowns occur. Tech breaks. Accidents happen. People get sick. These situations are perfect opportunities to strengthen your figureoutable muscles.

But if you want to supercharge your ability to overcome obstacles, reduce stress, and create outstanding results . . .

Go beyond yourself. Think in terms of *we*, not *me*.

You believing and behaving as though everything is figureoutable will radically change your life. But when the people around you—

friends, family, and colleagues—*also* believe and behave as though everything is figureoutable, you'll become capable of experiences and achievements beyond your wildest dreams.

First, it's way more fun to solve problems and overcome challenges together. Second, a community you can count on instantly multiplies the mental, emotional, spiritual, and creative resources available. Third, you're more likely to persevere in the face of setbacks when you have the support of others. Plus, the collaborative mix of ideas, strengths, and diverse perspectives often leads to far greater, richer results rooted in a deeper sense of purpose.

This quote by Martin Rutte perfectly illustrates the paradox we must all embrace:

"You have to do it by yourself, and you can't do it alone."

Yes, the only person you can control in life is you, and you must take full responsibility for the state of your life. Always and in all ways.

And . . .

We humans need each other. It's wired into our biology. No one exists on an island. Read biographies and investigate the subtle details in anyone's success story—you'll find that many souls played a supporting role in any single person's rise.

While the tools and tenets in this book apply to you as an individual, they don't end there. If you want the best chance to figure out your dreams, build a nourishing environment around you. Make it a priority to strengthen your social connections. Invest in others by caring and supporting their ability to figure out their dreams, too.

This isn't just feel-good fluff. Decades of research confirm the impact of positive social connections on our health, happiness, and performance. People with strong social connections have lower levels of anxiety and depression. They have higher self-esteem, are more empathetic, trusting, and cooperative with others. As a result, others are more trusting and cooperative with them.[1] The flip side is also true. One landmark study showed a *lack* of social connections is more harmful to your health than smoking, obesity, and high-blood pressure.[2] In fact, loneliness is as lethal as smoking fifteen cigarettes a day.[3]

Here's the good news: The strength of your social connections is something within your control. Like everything else, it's figureoutable.

BUILD YOUR FIGUREOUTABLE FORCE FIELD

If you want to lift yourself up, lift up someone else.
Booker T. Washington

If you recently stopped drinking, would you go to happy hour every day after work? If you were recovering from a gambling addiction, would you vacation in Vegas? If you recently discovered you were lactose intolerant, would you apply for a job in a cheese shop? Not a chance.

Why? Because your environment has enormous influence over the way you think, feel, and behave. Over time, your environment can make or break your success. That's why it's *so* important to take the lead and shape your environment—which includes the people you choose to spend time with—with intention and care.

The goal is to create a figureoutable force field, an ever-expanding ecosystem filled with supportive, kind people. One where everyone feels loved and respected for who they are. Here are three steps to get started.

1. INVEST IN FIGUREOUTABLE FRIENDS

Dr. Mark Hyman once told me, "Friend power is more important than willpower." It's hard to change your behavior or way of thinking if friends or loved ones aren't supportive. That's why you must be proactive. Share what you learned here with your closest friends. Give them a copy of this book. Talk about your ideas over coffee, cocktails, or a meal. Make the figureoutable philosophy part of your shared lexicon. Help each other "start before you're ready" and remember to focus on "progress not perfection."

If you're someone who's more into structure and accountability, this may inspire you. A study by the Association for Talent Development found that you've got a 65 percent chance of completing a goal if you commit to someone. Add a specific accountability appointment and you'll increase your chances of success by up to 95 percent. Yes, 95 percent!

Even without hard-core accountability, having friends you can count on is invaluable. When I find myself in a shit pickle, I call friends and colleagues. Whether it's work, relationship, or health related—I have no shame in reaching out and saying, "I know this is figureoutable, but I'm having a hard time seeing which way to go. Can we talk it through?"

The reason I can do that is because I invest in my friendships. Nothing is more important to me than my relationships. I do my best to be a proactive source of love, encouragement, and support for my friends' dreams, and you can do the same.

2. BE A FIGUREOUTABLE FORCE FOR GOOD AT WORK

Here's what it looks like in our company. A code red happens. A few text messages are exchanged. Once we realize we've got a significant problem on our hands, someone announces, "Something's effed up! Let's hop on a call to figure it out!" And we do. Every. Single. Time.

As adults, we spend the vast majority of our waking lives at work. No matter what your position (entry-level, freelancer, coordinator, manager, or CEO), commit to being a leader who believes and behaves as though everything is figureoutable. Show up in every environment with your figureoutable muscles flexed and ready. Say those words whenever you hit a problem, then back it up with action.

When your team hits an obstacle, be the first to say, "Hey, this is tough, but everything is figureoutable. We're capable and, if we work together, we *will* figure this out." That clear, calm, confident presence will have a positive ripple effect on your team. It will also help shift the focus away from stress, blame, and upset (all toxic and unproductive states, especially during a crisis) and toward creating a solution.

As Marianne Williamson reminds us, "An idea grows stronger when it's shared." If you lead a business, organization, or department, gift this book to everyone on your team. If you're a teacher or a coach, make *everything is figureoutable* a core lesson. Take the initiative to embed the figureoutable philosophy in your culture. We on Team Forleo use the ideas and tools from this book daily. I'm proud to say that folks regularly talk about having their "dream job" in our company. They even spend time together *outside* of work hours. I'm always hearing about team members meeting up on their vacations. No company is perfect, but ours is incredibly productive, caring, and supportive. I believe that's largely because the figureoutable philosophy is our foundation.

3. BECOME AN MF INSIDER TO GET ENDLESS FIGUREOUTABLE ENCOURAGEMENT FROM YOURS TRULY

The media and messages you consume are part of your mental and emotional ecosystem. What you read and listen to shapes your feelings, perspective, and behavior. If you've enjoyed this book, I'd love to continue supporting you on your journey.

We've been sharing free, award-winning content with our MF insiders (our email subscribers) every Tuesday for nearly two decades. Often, we send a new episode of *MarieTV* or *The Marie Forleo Podcast*. Sometimes it's a short, personal love note that makes your inbox smile. No matter what, you have my word: our content is uplifting, entertaining, and actionable. Everything we share will help you master the figureoutable philosophy and use your gifts to change the world. I'm proud to say that we have *thousands* of notes from subscribers who say that ours is the only email they read and look forward to each week.

Go to MarieForleo.com/EIF and enter your details. You'll get instant access to bonus material and additional training that didn't make its way into the book.

Whether it's with friends, colleagues, or loved ones, remember this golden relationship rule: whatever you long for, give to others.

If you long for more support, support others.

If you long for more appreciation, appreciate others.

If you long for more love and acceptance, love and accept others.

If you long for more recognition, recognize others.

If you long for more celebration, celebrate others.

If you long for more understanding, understand others.

Whenever you feel a sense of lack or that you "need" something, that's the exact moment to turn around and give it to someone else. Please know, you cannot do this as a manipulation. You can't give with an expectation of getting something back, because then it's no longer a gift but a demand. Instead, realize that which you give freely, you receive instantly. Whatever you give to another, you experience yourself.

Ultimately, the measure of our lives is not determined by what we achieve for ourselves; it's determined by what we share, give, and contribute to others. Do whatever you can to put yourself in an environment that focuses on contribution, not complaint. Giving, not getting. Service, not self-importance.

One last favor. **Promise me you'll keep going.** You're a precious soul with so much to create and contribute to this world.

Yes, I know. You're already juggling a lot. While you have some incredibly beautiful blessings (we all do), you're also navigating some challenges, too. Tough times don't come out of nowhere. They come precisely when you're ready to grow and be more of who you really are. You're stronger and more capable than you know.

Write to me and keep me posted on your growth. I'd love to hear how you're using what you've discovered here to change your life.

Till then, be good to yourself. You are your most important asset in this life. Remember to laugh and have fun, too.

Stay on your game and keep going for your dreams. Because the world really does need that special gift that *only* you have.

With all my love,
Marie
Venice Beach, California, March 2019

Never doubt that a small group of thoughtful, committed citizens can change the world; indeed, it's the only thing that ever has.

Margaret Mead

ACKNOWLEDGMENTS

The greatest and most fulfilling achievements in my life were not accomplished by me alone. Everything good and beautiful I've ever created, including this book, is connected to countless others. It's from the priceless contribution, collaboration, and encouragement of brilliant humans I have the honor of knowing.

To my beloved Josh, your relentless love, wisdom, and funny-ass adventurous spirit are treasures. Thank you for always believing in me. Thank you for seeing my potential, especially when I can't see it myself. I adore doing life with you. I love you more than you know.

To Team Forleo—the most magical badass crew in the world—including Tana, Geada, Louise, Marian (book wife!), Justin (Jams), Chelsea, Caroline, Sally, Kelsey, Audrey, Stevie, Erica, Meg, Mandy, Hailey, Heather H., Laura, Heather F., Meika, Jen, Ariel, Julia, Rachel, Sarah, Gregory, Elsa, Eric Michael, Josh B., Jason, and every glorious member of our wise, wild, creative, big-hearted ever-growing family, I bow to you. I worship you. Team Forleo is my ride or die for life.

To family, friends, and colleagues who continue to support me endlessly, Ronny, Zane, Ida, Jen and Zach, Juan and Bill, Kris Carr aka my best friend in the Universe, Regena Thomashauer, Laura Belgray, Gabby

Bernstein, Kate Northrup, Amy Porterfield, Sheila Kelley, Danielle La-Porte, Billy Beck III, Ophira Edut, Danielle Vieth, Grasie Mercedes, Damien Fahey, Seth Godin, Liz Gilbert, Sarah Jones, Dani Shapiro, Tony Robbins, Glennon Doyle, Brené Brown, Cheryl Strayed, Steve Pressfield, Simon Sinek, Tim Ferriss, Shawn Achor, Chris Guillebeau, Brendon Burchard, Kristin Loberg, Ryan Holiday—the pep talks, texts, meals, emails, advice, love, and support—your work, leadership, and friendship fuels me.

To my agent Bonnie Solow, I am so appreciative for your guidance and integrity.

To Adrian Zackheim, thank you for getting me and this idea, instantly. I adore you. To the entire Portfolio team including Leah Trouwborst, Chris Sergio, Will Weisser, Tara Gilbride, Lauren Monaco, Margot Stamas, Jessica Regione, Megan Gerrity, Matthew Boezi, Meighan Cavanaugh, Lillian Ball—thank you for your tireless efforts, heart, and care in bringing this baby to life.

To Oprah Winfrey, thank you for the extraordinary honor and joy of being invited on your show and stage. Since I was a little girl, you have been a beacon of possibility in my life. You continue to be one of my favorite humans, ever.

To our big, beautiful global community of *MarieTV* and *The Marie Forleo Podcast* fans, B-Schoolers, B-School Mentor Coaches, partners, Copy Cure students, our brilliant *MarieTV* guests, and the endless others I've connected with throughout the years—none of this would be possible without you.

To you, dear reader. I am so grateful for the generosity of your time, attention, and heart.

May you forever reach for your grandest dreams and highest hopes.

. . . and never, *ever* fucking give up.

APPENDIX

EVEN MORE
FIGUREOUTABLE
FIELD NOTES

We are the hero of our own story.
Mary McCarthy

After her financial aid was cut by 80 percent, she refused to be refused—and won over $16,000 in scholarships.

I decided to go back to school and pursue a degree in nutrition. I applied for financial aid and received a grant that covered my first year. I quit my administration job, started waiting tables, and began my journey.

The next year my financial aid was cut by 80 percent because I made *slightly* too much money waitressing. Of course, there was no way I could pay for school out of pocket and I couldn't pick up any more shifts since I was already struggling to juggle work and school. I felt defeated, like my dream was disappearing. That's when I saw a little talk given on Oprah's

SuperSoul Sessions where this amazing woman (that's you, Marie!) told me, "Everything is figureoutable." My life hasn't been the same since.

That quote got me thinking, "I can't quit now, that's ridiculous! This is figureoutable." I started researching ways to pay for school and decided scholarships would be the way to go. The majority of scholarships in my area all had deadlines approaching. I had two weeks to write and submit five "exceptional scholarship-winning" essays. All while in school and working a full-time job. Did I mention I have ADHD?

I figured it out by doing exactly what Marie prescribes (after I freaked out a little . . . or a lot). I dismantled the monster into small pieces. I took each essay, created an outline, and entered completion dates into my planner. I tackled them one by one, piece by piece, and finished three days before the deadline. I even had time for three people to proofread my work. Breaking the project down and putting it into my planner allowed me to (1) visually see that it was doable and (2) calm down and focus, allowing my creativity to flow instead of being in a state of perpetual self-doubt.

As a result, I was awarded the following amounts in scholarship funds: $12,000, $2,000, $1,500, $800!

Everything is figureoutable is my foundation. It's my blankie when things seem overwhelming. I say it out loud. I believe it. I'm not afraid anymore because it has repeatedly proven to be The Truth . . . EVERYTHING IS FIGUREOUTABLE. Thank you, Marie. You changed my life and touched my heart. I appreciate you more than words could ever say.

—CARRIE
TEXAS

After delaying his artistic dreams for sixteen years,
this engineer quit his job and figured out how to earn
a living through his art.

I desperately wanted to quit my corporate career and become a full-time artist. I had been creating art since childhood but instead of going to art school I studied engineering and spent sixteen years working in manufacturing and IT. I was creating art along the way, but craved more. My wife and whole family supported me when I eventually decided to quit my job. I had no idea how I was going to support us, but I told myself, "Everything is figureoutable!"

I accepted a part-time teaching opportunity at a management college, earning just enough to stay afloat and pay my studio rent. I started teaching Ganapati idol-making workshops and other art workshops on the side. I wanted to offer these classes in the US, but it wasn't practical or feasible since I live in India.

Then a friend introduced me to online teaching. I immediately decided to make an online course about how to make a Ganapati idol. It was tough and I had to figure out many things about video recording, lighting, editing, audio, and marketing, but I'm happy I did. The class was a hit! My course was covered in the local media and it's still the only course on this topic anywhere on the internet. I was hooked. I now have twenty-five online courses and my paintings are in personal and corporate collections in more than seven countries. Everything is figureoutable!

—MANDAR
INDIA

"When love is your motivation, everything is figureoutable."

My grandfather passed away unexpectedly. He lived in England. I live in Kalamazoo, Michigan. I had a two-year-old and a two-month-old, a business, and a busy husband/business partner. The funeral was set for Thursday at 11:00 a.m. in a small village outside Manchester. Every fiber in my being told me that I had to be there, but as a nursing mama, I HAD to bring my baby . . .

The mantra "Everything is figureoutable" got me through:

- Rearranging schedules for my entire family.
- Finding last-minute daycare for my toddler.
- Finding the funds to buy a last-minute plane ticket.
- 2:00 a.m. packing, prepping, and pumping sessions.

And then . . . things got really hard. *Everything is figureoutable* got me through:

- A delayed flight and missed connection.
- An unexpected sleepover in a snowstorm in Detroit with my two-month-old baby.
- Being told, "I'm sorry, the earliest we can get you into Manchester is Thursday EVENING." (Oh HELL no.)

Everything is figureoutable is what gave me the courage to stand strong. Speak up. Switch airlines. Find a new path. Land in Manchester Airport at 7:00 a.m. Thursday. Get a ride to his small village on time and with one hour to spare. All on no sleep with my baby girl strapped to me. I have never been more proud of myself. And of my family. Here's how I figured it out:

- Deep breaths.
- Literally telling the Delta agents, "Everything is figureoutable!"
- Lots of phone calls.
- Never taking no for an answer.
- Being open to flying to unexpected places in order to get to my final destination.

I made it to my grandfather's funeral. I was able to say my final goodbye to a man who meant the world to me. I was able to hold my baby girl while we buried him in the same cemetery where generations of my ancestors are buried. I showed myself, my children, and my extended family that when love is your motivation, everything is figureoutable.

—KATE

MICHIGAN

This full-time teacher uses everything is figureoutable *on both the tiniest tasks and her biggest, scariest obstacles.*

Marie's (and her mom's) mantra "Everything is figureoutable" has shifted me and continues to do so in such a powerful way. It's challenging to land on just one problem this mantra has helped with because it comes up for me daily, often bubbling up over and over again.

Whether it's the panic that comes right after I've realized I've lost my wallet or the angst I feel when my rent is due—this is figureoutable. Trains not running properly on a weekend and I'm now running late—this is figureoutable. Balancing being a full-time teacher in a high-performing low-income school, launching a yoga retreat business, writing a book, and making time for human connection and self-development—this is figure-outable.

This mantra helps me face the tiniest of tasks and the biggest, scariest obstacles. It has been so instrumental in my life that I've made it my pass-word. Typing in "figureoutable" multiple times a day gives me a sense of calm and courage to take on a rich and full life.

Once I remind myself that everything is figureoutable, I'm calmer and clearheaded enough to take action. The first step usually involves making a list or reaching out for help. The end result is that I always figure it out. My rent is paid, I've learned the trains in a new city, I've learned how to embed a payment form on my website, etc. I'm still in the midst of many figureoutable moments, but Marie's mantra provides me with the reassur-ance and permission to move forward.

—KATYA

NEW YORK

Everything is figureoutable *helped this working mom of two survive her husband's deployment.*

My husband was leaving for a six-month deployment and I had to figure out how to hold down the fort with two kids and a full-time job without losing my sanity. I wanted to face one of the most difficult challenges of my life and come out stronger and healthier on the other side.

The mantra "Everything is figureoutable" gave me confidence to be-lieve that—in spite of the loneliness, the heaviness, and the overwhelm—I could totally crush these six months apart. It helped me to choose fight over flight, and strength over survival. When I was afraid of the dark every single night, I figured it out. When I had to shoulder the taxes, the parenting, the housekeeping, and the work-life balance, I figured it out. When lightning struck the only tree in my front yard and it fell on top of our car, I figured it out (after I cried a little).

When I knew that my husband would be leaving, it felt like a staggering impossibility to maintain a normal existence without him. The thought alone gave me anxiety! So I figured out a way to get some help. I asked our babysitter and college student extraordinaire to take the guest bedroom and live with us rent-free in exchange for help with the kids and keeping me company. Her presence made our lives so much more bearable and even fun! (Holla at ya, Becca!)

I took mundane tasks one day at a time and learned to have a tremendous amount of grace with myself. Sometimes it's way more important to figure out self-care than how to squeeze in the laundry and the dishes on a work night! I also figured out how to ask my neighbors and friends for help rather than curl up into a ball of defeat. (Lookin' at you, tree car.)

Perhaps one of the most impactful things I figured out was how to care for myself so that I could take care of everything else on my plate. I signed up with a personal trainer and got help with my nutrition. I bought a bike and focused on doing things I loved so I could be renewed and energized instead of drained and used up.

The end result was that I survived the six-month deployment with my sanity intact. I strengthened my friendships and made new ones. Everything is figureoutable, and I'm so glad that someone told me so.

—KAYLA

MISSOURI

"Marie's mantra is their mantra as well as mine, and I know they will pass it on to their children in the future."

One day my car tire was nearly flat and I had no clue what to do. I remembered Marie's mantra and Googled my car model and tire air pressure at the gas station and sorted out my flat tire in two minutes. This gave me proof and confidence that everything IS figureoutable.

I've since gone on to get a well-paying job and run my own business on the side. I have a range of power tools and my very own toolbox to flip a new four-bedroom house by the sea in Ireland. I passed Marie's mantra on through word and action to my four children. Three of them have flown the coop and are studying law, accountancy, and psychology and all living and working independently from me without a single loan. Marie's mantra is their mantra as well as mine and I know they will pass it on to their children in the future.

—ELLEN
IRELAND

She used everything is figureoutable *to give herself the courage to escape a dangerous relationship and start a new life.*

I was in a relationship I never should've been in to begin with. All the red flags were there, but I ignored them. One night, after months of awful fights, it came to an ugly and scary head. I needed to pack everything I owned—an entire house full of furniture, my office, and two sweet pups—and get it all into storage by the end of the next day.

By this time, I knew the phrase "Everything is figureoutable," so I repeated it over and over. I repeated it on the phone to friends who were scared to death for me. I repeated it to the movers who showed up within two hours to pack me up. To a neighbor who took time out of her day to help me pack my most precious belongings. All day long I repeated, "Everything is figureoutable."

It was an awful, awful nine months leading up to this moment, but it led to the happiest of endings because I controlled my thought process with this one phrase. It helped me keep going because I had no time to stop and freak out.

I broke everything down step by step. First, I called the police to be sure I was safe. Then I searched online for last-minute movers (I had no idea, but they exist, thank goodness). Then I rented a storage unit. Then I had my cousin, a lawyer, draw up a letter. In between I packed boxes, the movers showed up, and it was all out and in storage by six that night. I still get chills thinking about it. And I'm still so proud of how well it went and how strong I was/am.

I still use *everything is figureoutable* today. I moved back to Texas, met the man of my dreams, and got married. We now live in a beautiful house in California and I'm working on a project I truly believe in.

—JULIA
CALIFORNIA

"On the anniversary of my mama's passing, everything is figureoutable *brought the light back into my heart."*

After my mom passed away I lost my entire sense of direction. I had lost my dad at nineteen, and now I was an orphan. My mom was my closest friend and her passing left me feeling like I'd lost my lighthouse and was stumbling in the darkness. Nothing felt like it would ever be figureoutable again.

On the anniversary of my mama's passing, "Everything Is Figureoutable" arrived in my inbox and Marie brought the light back into my heart. It was not one specific solution to a specific problem, it was a complete transformation of spirit. My heart extended. My eyes opened to the world again, and I felt my soul come alive as the wisdom sank into my bones.

This is what I had been doing every day, even when I felt like I was crumbling and could not face another day. I chose to show up . . . for my partner, for my children, and above all, for myself. "Everything is figureoutable" continues to be my daily mantra. It is the key message (along with choosing kindness and respect) that I model for my kids, and it is a message I now hear them repeat to their friends.

Marie and I have never met, and yet in my darkest hour she opened me up to the person I am. Her message is the lighthouse. It is not about doing one thing differently, it is a complete way of living and being in the world . . . every single day. In the darkness, in the shadows, and even in the brightest sun. Through the joys and the heartache, everything is figureoutable. Always.

—PATRYCJA
QUEBEC

Everything is figureoutable *helped her revisit a long-forgotten novel with a fresh perspective.*

A long while back, I started a novel. I was a young mom experiencing the challenges that present themselves at that particular time. In addition to raising three little ones, we were dealing with a parent in the throes of Alzheimer's. After a walk through a cemetery and seeing my name on a tombstone, I wrote a short story, which ultimately morphed into an outline for a novel in the genre of magic realism.

Over the next few years, I pursued and earned a doctorate, which necessitated putting everything else aside. Soon after beginning B-School, I made the decision to revisit the novel. Although I still felt passionate about the theme, it just wasn't working in its original iteration. I felt so discouraged because I'd made a commitment to finishing it once I'd earned my degree.

I went back to the keyboard, but after days staring at old words and blank pages, I happened upon Marie's Oprah talk. Amazingly, it unleashed a flood of ideas.

I realized that the block I was experiencing was a result of being a different person today than when I first wrote the short story. Once I was open to the process without urgency or preconceived results, I found the answers. I introduced a new character and everything started to click—especially my keyboard! It is all a gift and it is all figureoutable! Insights for which I am incredibly grateful.

—LILLIAN

NEW YORK

She lobbied government to help her grandparents keep their only source of income.

Our state government made an announcement that they were canceling limousine licenses, simply throwing them in the bin. My grandparents, who are in their nineties, had five licenses and the lease on those licenses is their only source of income—a modest income, but it was all they needed. Which meant they were about to lose everything.

At the time, there were devastating stories of cab and limousine license owners and operators committing suicide. It devastated my grandfather. He was such a proud provider who worked so very hard to have assets he could leave to his nine children.

He was now too frail to look after his investments, so when the government made this announcement, the ball was in my court. I knew nothing about the industry and even less about politics (not even who my state member was!).

"It's all figureoutable," I told myself. I knew I could figure *this* out.

I took it one step at a time. I went to a limousine meeting for the first time in my life and voiced my concerns. Then I organized a meeting of others with the same concerns. Then I started an industry association. Then I organized protests and a social media campaign to get the government to even talk to me (they'd locked me out of everything).

I find that in figuring one thing out, there's such a flow effect. I now get super excited about the challenges I face because it's usually a stepping-stone to something greater. Eventually I appeared in the media, made submissions to parliamentary committees, and spoke to countless politicians. I did everything I could to influence change.

The government eventually renounced their decision—and my grandparents still have an income. I figured it out and then some!

My association is now the peak body, and I also sit on the Government's

Industry Reference Group. My desire to figure out how to help my grandad has, in turn, helped many others in the limousine industry in Queensland. I formed wonderful friendships and have learned so many new things. One senior government staffer even told me I should start teaching people how to lobby government!

I know everything is figureoutable, I was born knowing that. But I never had the words for it until Marie articulated it so well. Now, whenever I encounter challenges I can hear her saying, "Everything is figureoutable" and I go, "Yep, she's right, now let's get on with it."

—JACQUI
AUSTRALIA

NOTES

CHAPTER 1: THE TROPICANA ORANGE

1. Tristram Stuart, *Waste: Uncovering the Global Food Scandal* (New York: W. W. Norton, 2009).
2. "Ten Great Reasons to Give to Charity," The Life You Can Save, accessed March 15, 2019, https://www.thelifeyoucansave.org/learn-more/why-donate#collapseFAQs.

CHAPTER 3: THE MAGIC OF BELIEF

1. Walter A. Brown, "Expectation, the Placebo Effect and the Response to Treatment," *Rhode Island Medical Journal*, May 19, 2015, http://rimed.org/rimedicaljournal /2015/05/2015-05-19-cont-brown.pdf.
2. Ulrich W. Weger and Stephen Loughnan, "Mobilizing Unused Resources: Using the Placebo Concept to Enhance Cognitive Performance," *The Quarterly Journal of Experimental Psychology*, https://www.tandfonline.com/doi/figure/10.1080/17470218.2012 .751117.
3. *60 Minutes*, "Marva Collins 1995 Part 1," YouTube video, 7:56, https://www.youtube .com/watch?v=h8b1Behi9FM.
4. Alyssa Toomey, "Oprah Winfrey Talks Barbara Walters' Legacy," *E! News*, May 16, 2014, http://www.eonline.com/news/542751/oprah-winfrey-talks-barbara-walters -legacy-former-view-host-gets-teary-eyed-while-talking-about-her-final-show.
5. American Psychological Association, "Marriage and Divorce," https://www.apa.org /topics/divorce.

6. McKinley Irvin Family Law, "32 Shocking Divorce Statistics," https://www.mckin leyirvin.com/family-law-blog/2012/october/32-shocking-divorce-statistics.

CHAPTER 4: ELIMINATE EXCUSES

1. Victor Mather, "Bethany Hamilton, a Shark-Attack Survivor, Reaches an Unlikely Crest," *New York Times*, May 31, 2016, https://www.nytimes.com/2016/06/01/sports /bethany-hamilton-world-surf-league.html; "Learn About Bethany," BethanyHam ilton.com, https://bethanyhamilton.com/biography; "Bethany Hamilton Biography," *Biography*, https://www.biography.com/people/bethany-hamilton.

2. Tererai Trent, *The Awakened Woman: Remembering & Reigniting Our Sacred Dreams* (New York: Enliven/Atria, 2017); "Have an Impossible Dream? This Woman Proves You Can Achieve It," *MarieTV*, https://www.marieforleo.com/2019/03/tererai-trent -achieve-your-dreams.

3. Nicholas Kristof, "Triumph of a Dreamer," *New York Times*, November 14, 2009, https://www.nytimes.com/2009/11/15/opinion/15kristof.html; Nicholas D. Kristof and Sheryl WuDunn, *Half the Sky: Turning Oppression into Opportunity for Women Worldwide* (New York: Vintage Books, 2010); "A Remarkable Story," Tereraitrent.org, https://tereraitrent.org/about.

4. The author of this passage is questionable. While often attributed to pastor Chuck Swindoll, this quote appears in Nell W. Mohney's *Don't Put a Period Where God Put a Comma*. It's also attributed to Cosmas in *From Trials to Triumphs* by Ambassador Udo Moses Williams and Eno Udo Williams. Regardless of who said it, the sentiment is spot-on.

5. "Have an Impossible Dream?," *MarieTV*.

6. Nick Bilton, "Steve Jobs Was a Low-Tech Parent," *New York Times*, September 10, 2014, https://www.nytimes.com/2014/09/11/fashion/steve-jobs-apple-was-a-low-tech -parent.html.

7. S. Andrews, D. A. Ellis, H. Shaw, L. Piwek, and J. Pietsching, "Beyond Self-Report: Tools to Compare Estimated and Real-World Smartphone Use," *PLoS ONE* 10: 10, October 28, 2015, http://doi.org/10.1371/journal.pone.0139004.

8. "Cost of Attendance," NYU Langone Health, https://med.nyu.edu/education/md -degree/md-affordability-financial-aid/cost-attendance.

9. Medha Imam, "$2.9 Billion Unused Federal Grant Awards in Last Academic Year," *USA Today*, January 20, 2015, https://www.usatoday.com/story/college/2015/01/20/29 -billion-unused-federal-grant-awards-in-last-academic-year/37399897.

CHAPTER 5: HOW TO DEAL WITH THE FEAR OF ANYTHING

1. Alicia Eaton, *Fix Your Life with NLP* (New York: Simon & Schuster, 2013).

CHAPTER 6: DEFINE YOUR DREAM

1. Sandhya Bhaskar, "'There Is No Difference': Laverne Cox Talks Gender Identity in Memorial Hall," *The Panther*, March 4, 2019, http://www.thepantheronline.com /news/no-difference-laverne-cox-talks-gender-identity-memorial-hall.
2. Erin Staley, *Laverne Cox* (New York: The Rosen Publishing Group, 2017).
3. Jazz Jennings, "Laverne Cox," *Time*, April 15, 2015, http://time.com/3822970/laverne -cox-2015-time-100.
4. Brian McVicar, "'Orange Is the New Black' Actress Discusses 'Gender Police,' Struggles Faced by Transgender People," *MLive*, March 19, 2014, https://www.mlive.com /news/grand-rapids/2014/03/orange_is_the_new_black_actres_1.html.
5. Jane Mulkerrins, "Laverne Cox: On Growing Up Trans, Orange Is the New Black and Caitlyn Jenner," *Telegraph*, June 10, 2016, https://www.telegraph.co.uk/on-dem and/2016/06/10/laverne-cox-on-growing-up-trans-orange-is-the-new-black-and -cait.
6. "Laverne Cox at Creating Change 2014," National LGBTQ Task Force, February 5, 2014, YouTube video, 30:46, https://www.youtube.com/watch?v=6cytc0p4Jwg.
7. Mulkerrins, "Laverne Cox: On Growing Up Trans, Orange Is the New Black and Caitlyn Jenner."
8. Regan Reid, "10 Teachable Moments from Laverne Cox's Incredibly Inspiring Talk at WorldPride," *IndieWire*, June 26, 2014, https://www.indiewire.com/2014/06 /10-teachable-moments-from-laverne-coxs-incredibly-inspiring-talk-at-worldpride -213999.
9. Benjamin Lindsay, "Laverne Cox on Breaking Barriers in Hollywood & Advocating for the Marginalized," *Backstage*, March 8, 2017, https://www.backstage.com/maga zine/article/laverne-cox-breaking-barriers-hollywood-advocating-marginalized -5039.

CHAPTER 8: PROGRESS NOT PERFECTION

1. Alaska Injury Prevention Center; Critical Illness and Trauma Foundation, Inc., and American Association of Suicidology, "Alaska Suicide Follow-back Study Final Report," September 1, 2003–August 31, 2006, http://dhss.alaska.gov/SuicidePreven tion/Documents/pdfs_sspc/sspcfollowback2-07.pdf.

2. Prem S. Fry and Dominique L. Debats, "Perfectionism and the Five-Factor Personality Traits as Predictors of Mortality in Older Adults," *Journal of Health Psychology* 14, no. 4 (2009), 513–24, doi:10.1177/1359105309103571.

3. Fry and Debats, "Perfectionism and the Five-Factor Personality Traits"; Gordon L. Flett and Paul L. Hewitt, "Perfectionism and Maladjustment: An Overview of Theoretical, Definitional, and Treatment Issues," in *Perfectionism: Theory, Research, and Treatment,* ed. Gordon L. Flett and Paul L. Hewitt (Washington, DC: American Psychological Association, 2002), 5, http://dx.doi.org/10.1037/10458-001.

4. Ira Glass, "The Gap," produced by Daniel Sax, *This American Life,* January 25, 2014, https://www.thisamericanlife.org/extras/the-gap.

5. Carol Dweck, *Mindset: The New Psychology of Success* (New York: Random House, 2006).

CHAPTER 9: REFUSE TO BE REFUSED

1. Seth Godin, *This Is Marketing* (Portfolio: New York, 2018).

CHAPTER 10: THE WORLD NEEDS YOUR SPECIAL GIFT

1. Jaruwan Sakulku, "The Impostor Phenomenon," *International Journal of Behavioral Science* 6, no. 1 (2011), https://www.tci-thaijo.org/index.php/IJBS/article/view/521.

2. Brené Brown, "Finding Shelter in a Shame Storm (and Avoiding the Flying Debris)," Oprah.com, http://www.oprah.com/spirit/brene-brown-how-to-conquer-shame -friends-who-matter/al.

EPILOGUE: THE REAL SECRET TO LASTING SUCCESS

1. Richard M. Lee and Steven B. Robbins, "The Relationship Between Social Connectedness and Anxiety, Self-Esteem, and Social Identity," *Journal of Counseling Psychology* 45, no. 3 (1998), 338–45, http://dx.doi.org/10.1037/0022-0167.45.3.338.

2. J. S. House, K. R. Landis, and D. Umberson, "Social Relationships and Health," *Science* 241, no. 4865 (1988), 540–45, http://science.sciencemag.org/content/241/4865/540.

3. Savada Chandra Tiwari, "Loneliness: A Disease?," *Indian Journal of Psychiatry* 55, no. 4 (2013), 320–22, https://www.ncbi.nlm.nih.gov/pmc/articles/PMC3890922.

INDEX

Note: Page numbers in *italics* refer to tables or illustrations.

INDEX

Remember that gal that gave up?
Neither does anyone else.

Unknown

PENGUIN PARTNERSHIPS

Penguin Partnerships is the Creative Sales and Promotions team at Penguin Random House. We have a long history of working with clients on a wide variety of briefs, specializing in brand promotions, bespoke publishing and retail exclusives, plus corporate, entertainment and media partnerships.

We can respond quickly to briefs and specialize in repurposing books and content for sales promotions, for use as incentives and retail exclusives as well as creating content for new books in collaboration with our partners as part of branded book relationships.

Equally if you'd simply like to buy a bulk quantity of one of our existing books at a special discount, we can help with that too. Our books can make excellent corporate or employee gifts.

Special editions, including personalized covers, excerpts of existing books or books with corporate logos can be created in large quantities for special needs.

We can work within your budget to deliver whatever you want, however you want it.

For more information, please contact
salesenquiries@penguinrandomhouse.co.uk